ICT in the Primary School

ICT in the Primary School
From Pedagogy to Practice

Gary Beauchamp

Harlow, England • London • New York • Boston • San Francisco • Toronto • Sydney • Auckland • Singapore • Hong Kong
Tokyo • Seoul • Taipei • New Delhi • Cape Town • São Paulo • Mexico City • Madrid • Amsterdam • Munich • Paris • Milan

Pearson Education Limited
Edinburgh Gate
Harlow
Essex CM20 2JE
England

and Associated Companies throughout the world

Visit us on the World Wide Web at:
www.pearson.com/uk

First published 2012

ISBN: 978-1-4082-5136-2

British Library Cataloguing-in-Publication Data
A catalogue record for this book is available from the British Library

Library of Congress Cataloging-in-Publication Data
A catalog record for this book is available from the British Library

10 9 8 7 6 5 4 3 2 1
16 15 14 13 12

Typeset in in 9.75/12pt Giovanni Book by 71
Printed and bound by Ashford Colour Press Ltd., Gosport

This book is dedicated to Janet, Owen, Elin, Bob, Jean and Bill who, in different ways, have provided encouragement, ideas, support and belief.

Contents

Acknowledgements

Author's acknowledgements

I have been fortunate to work with many people who have developed my thinking on the use of ICT in education. In particular, I would like to acknowledge the influence of Dr Steve Kennewell, who has provided advice, academic rigour and necessary caution. Also, colleagues from Swansea University and UWIC have both challenged and supported me over the years. As a result many of the ideas in this book are the product of debate, experiment and argument from a team, rather than any individual. In addition, I would also like to acknowledge the helpful suggestions of reviewers at various stages in the production of the book. Having said all this, any mistakes or omissions in this book remain my responsibility.

Publisher's acknowledgements

We are grateful to the following for permission to reproduce copyright material:

Figures

Figure 6.1 from Progression in primary ICT, David Fulton (Bennett, R., Hamill, A. and Pickford, T. 2007) Routledge, From: Progression in primary ICT, Bennett, R., Hamill, A. and Pickford, T. Copyright © 2007, David Fulton. Reproduced by permission of Taylor & Francis Books UK; Figure 8.2 from Graphicacy for life, Primary Geographer, June pp.6-8 (Mackintosh, M. 2011), The Geographical Association, www.geography.org.uk

Tables

Table 3.2 adapted from The Instructional Design Knowledge Base, http://classweb.gmu.edu/ndabbagh/Resources/IDKB/models_theories.htm, Nada Dabbagh, Dabbagh, N. The Instructional Design Knowledge Base. Available from http://classweb.gmu.edu/ndabbagh/Resources/IDKB/index.htm; Table 6.2 from Dialogue table, http://dialogueiwb.educ.cam.ac.uk/resources/, Sara Hennessy, None; Table 7.1 from The key stage 1 curriculum http://curriculum.qcda.gov.uk/key-stages-1-and-2/subjects/index.aspx, National Curriculum, Crown Copyright material is reproduced with permission under the terms of the Click-Use Licence

Text

Extract on page 103 from OFSTED (2009) Mathematics: understanding the score: Improving practice in mathematics teaching at primary level. London: OFSTED., © Crown Copyright; Extract on page 104 from OFSTED (2009) Mathematics: understanding the score: Improving practice in mathematics teaching at primary level, p.12. London: OFSTED., © Crown Copyright

Photos

The publisher would like to thank the following for their kind permission to reproduce their photographs: p.75 Talking Products Ltd; p.76 Shutterstock.com.

In some instances we have been unable to trace the owners of copyright material, and we would appreciate any information that would enable us to do so.

CHAPTER 1

What is ICT in the Primary School?: Tools and Techniques

In this chapter we will examine the key reasons for why we should use ICT in the primary school to allow pupils and teachers to work together in learning experiences. We will then examine the unique features of ICT and capabilities of ICT and how these can be used in lessons.

Introduction

It was a relatively short time ago that Information and Communications Technology (ICT) took its place in the curriculum of the primary school. As well as becoming a subject in the curriculum, however, ICT in the primary school has assumed a life of its own as a 'complex tool which can be used by teachers and by pupils in teaching and learning'. (Higgins, 2001, p164) As part of this development, teachers have had to develop practical ICT skills both during their training and throughout their career. As hardware and software develop, the skills required also change and any book which deals with specific hardware resources or software packages is often out of date very quickly. What changes less quickly, and is arguably more important, is the pedagogic thinking which underpins the use of both hardware and software by both pupils and teachers. This book is primarily concerned with the latter and is not intended to equip you with practical ICT skills, but to allow you to critically explore the fundamental principles behind how ICT can be used in developing effective teaching and learning in early years (EY) settings and primary schools. This exploration will be based upon evidence from research and practical experience gained in a wide range of learning settings. Although part of this exploration will help address some Qualified Teacher Status (QTS) standards, the main intention is to examine how ICT can be used as an effective pedagogic tool at any point in your career.

The introduction of technology, such as the interactive whiteboard (IWB), into the classroom, as well as technological advances allowing personal computers (PCs) and other mobile devices to become faster, smaller and easier to use, has been rapid. As John and Sutherland (2005, p406) point out, 'in recent years the emergence of new digital technologies has offered up the possibility of extending and deepening classroom learning in ways hitherto unimagined'. These possibilities have ensured that opportunities and challenges have presented themselves to teacher and pupils in equal measure. One of the most important advances has been in the increased availability and speed of access to the internet, which, together with other advances in mobile and other technologies, has enabled the development of e-learning opportunities. Definitions of e-learning vary and Mayes and de Freitas (2007, p13) go so far as to suggest that 'there are really no models of e-learning *per se* – only e-enhancements of existing models of learning'. In this book we will examine a range of such enhancements but, given the pervasive(and contested) nature of e-learning, we will adopt Holmes and Gardner's (2006, p14) simple definition as 'online access to learning resources, anywhere and anytime'.

Alongside technical developments, there have been changes in thinking about education in general terms, specifically in the early years and more generally in the role pupils play in their own learning. In 2009, the 'Rose Review' (DCSF, 2009, p9) concluded that 'primary children relish learning independently and co-operatively'. Although the report itself was ultimately rejected, research evidence examined below will show that such an approach remains beneficial. In this context, the roles of teachers and learners have evolved to reflect greater autonomy for pupils and a more facilitating role for teachers. In other words, education is not something that is done *to* children, but is something that is done *with* them as active partners who are able to influence the course of the lesson.

Many advocates of ICT in education would share this view and adopt a socio-cultural perspective in which learning is situated and socially constructed. (Vygotsky, 1978) Beauchamp and Kennewell (2010) suggest that the classroom is an ecology of resources, defined by Luckin (2008, p451) as 'a set of inter-related resource elements, including people and objects, the interactions between which provide a particular context'. This perspective will be considered in more detail in Chapter 2, but at this stage it is important to note that a key part of a socio-cultural perspective is the assertion that 'tools', both 'technical' and 'cognitive', play a central role in mediating human action. Although language remains the most important cultural tool, other tools can include paper, books, pens and, of course, ICT resources. It is the ability of ICT to provide a range of tools (such as the IWB, digital camera or mobile phone) in one place that makes it such an important means of mediating learning. However, as Wertsch (1991, p. 119 cited in Gillen et al., 2008) points out it is 'only by being part of action [that] mediational means come into being and play their role. They have no magical power in and of themselves'. In other words, the ICT tool(s) need to actively involved in achieving both activity and outcomes in lessons; just using them is not enough. It is also important that all people are involved in their use. If we return to the idea that learning is socially constructed, we see the importance of everyone in the classroom using ICT to construct (and even deconstruct) knowledge and understanding. A belief that pupils should assume some responsibility for, and control over, their learning, would also apply to the use of the relevant 'tools'. As part of this process, ICT has evolved from being a subject that was taught by teachers to learners, or a resource or tool 'owned' by the teacher, to become a shared resource/tool for learning and teaching by both. Such a change requires teachers to examine both their pedagogic beliefs and classroom practice, especially how they plan and use ICT in learning.

This change in 'ownership' of ICT and its implications will be discussed in more detail in Chapter 2, but before this I want you to imagine arriving at school (early of course!) and finding the classroom projector bulb has blown and the internet connection is not working. Worst still, you have forgotten your memory device with all your resources for lessons on. Could you still teach effective lessons? The answer, of course, is yes which poses the question: do we really need ICT in the primary school and early years settings? It may seem somewhat strange to start a book about ICT by asking this fundamental question, but in addressing it we begin to identify *why* we should use ICT, *how* and *when it* should be used, and *who* should use it to best improve learning and teaching. In this first chapter, we will begin with looking at *why* we really do need ICT.

Why use ICT?

Potential for positive impact on learning

The first, and perhaps most important, reason for using ICT is that it *can* have a positive effect on attainment. Cox et al., (2003, p3) undertook a comprehensive review of research and concluded that 'evidence from the literature shows the positive effects of specific uses of ICT on pupils' attainment in almost all the National Curriculum subjects'. This claim is, however, immediately qualified by stating that 'there is a strong relationship between the ways in which ICT has been used and pupils' attainment. This suggests that the crucial component in the appropriate selection and use of ICT within education is the teacher and his or her pedagogical approaches.' Although this does not take account of the impact of pupils' input into the process, it does underline the need for teachers to be aware of the full range of ICT's capabilities from which they can select the most appropriate uses. Indeed, it is important to realise that just using ICT does not mean it will have a positive impact. As Somekh and Davies (1999, p153) conclude, 'computers, of themselves, are not transforming'. In the years since, it seems probable that the same applies to the wider range of ICT resources now available. In a broader sense, this is supported by John and Sutherland (2005, p406), who assert that 'in reality, learning is always distributed in some form between the technology, the learner and the context and there is nothing inherent in technology that automatically guarantees learning'. This theme is developed by Cox et al., (2003, p4) who contend that many studies 'show that insufficient understanding of the scope of an ICT resource leads to inappropriate or superficial uses in the curriculum'. Thus to ensure effective use in learning and teaching, teachers must have a fully developed understanding of the features of ICT before they decide how and when to apply them or when to allow pupils to use them.

Unique features of ICT

ICT can offer a range of unique features to teachers and learners which are not available using other means. Although the range of ICT equipment is wide, the following general features are strengths of ICT:

- *Speed*: making processes happen more quickly than other methods.
- *Automation*: making previously tedious or effortful processes happen automatically (other than changing the form of representation).
- *Capacity*: the storage and retrieval of large amounts of material.

- *Range*: access to materials in different forms and from a wider range of sources than otherwise possible.
- *Provisionality*: the facility to change content, and change back if necessary.
- *Interactivity*: the ability to respond to user input repeatedly.

(Kennewell and Beauchamp, 2007)

It is worth considering each of these factors in turn and examining how they may apply to specific hardware and software. As already stated, this book is not a 'how to' guide to hardware and software, so any examples will be generic. They will also primarily relate to teacher use of ICT, but later chapters will consider the importance of allowing pupils to use ICT as a tool for learning.

Speed

ICT can make things happen very fast. Whilst this may be useful at times, for example to gain attention or add pace to a lesson, it should be used with care. As a teacher, it is very useful to be able to move quickly through a prepared series of images, or examples from texts, to present an idea in a variety of contexts or different forms of presentation. For the learner, however, this may not always be beneficial. Although ICT allows things to happen quickly, the teacher remains central to the *control* of this speed, guided by the needs of the learners. The analogy of an accelerator pedal in a car is useful. No driver would keep their foot on of the accelerator without being aware of the conditions around them, any more than a teacher would present information to learners without being aware of the needs and reactions of their pupils. Speed as a feature applies to all ICT devices, but an example in this case would be the interactive whiteboard (IWB). This allows teachers, and indeed pupils in a synergistic classroom (Beauchamp, 2004), to move from slide to slide, image to image or between programs very quickly. The dual nature of ICT as a resource for teachers **and** pupils will be considered in detail in later chapters, but here we need to note the importance of the teacher in ensuring that speed is not used at the expense of understanding, whoever is using the ICT.

Automation

At the same time, however, this speedy movement through prepared resources (such as a PowerPoint or other file) demonstrates the feature of automation. Before the advent of ICT resources, such as the interactive whiteboard (IWB), teachers would have to produce text in real time (often with their back to the class) or to try and illustrate an example with a poster or a drawing. Automation allows teachers to produce whole pages of text or complicated diagrams at the touch of a screen or mouse. The benefits of automation may perhaps be better recognised when something goes wrong with the computer or projectors in the classroom and you have to return to writing things on a traditional black/whiteboard or using handheld posters instead of high quality graphics on the IWB!

WHAT DO YOU THINK?

A class teacher has prepared a PowerPoint for their class. This has taken a long time as it includes text, images and even a short movie. Half way through the lesson the teacher realises that the first few slides have provoked so much discussion that there is little chance of getting through all the rest of the presentation as originally planned – including some good pictures and the movie. Due to the speed and automation features of ICT, the teacher knows that it is possible to get through all the slides. Should the teacher use these features to finish the slideshow? What are the possible implications of doing so?

Capacity

Automation would be of limited use without the ability to store large amounts of information. There have been rapid advances in recent years ago in the ability to the store and retrieve information quickly. Another important recent development is that storage devices have become both smaller and cheaper. It is now possible to save and access a range of data, even large video files, from very small Storage Devices or networks (both wired and wireless). Many of these networks can be accessed from any classroom in a school, thus enabling the easy sharing and re-use of resources, or even from outside of school for teachers to work at home in preparing work. In recent times these networks have also become virtual and do not always need a wired connection, for example, through 'Cloud computing' – more to follow later. This enables files to be uploaded or even programs to be accessed, from anywhere with an internet connection – for example a teacher from home or on a trip away from a school. In addition to networks, the development of Web 2.0 technology has created other means of storing and, more importantly, adding new content so that pupils can become contributors as well as consumers. In reality, teachers are limited only by their imagination in choosing and using effectively a wide variety of content for lessons.

Range

Not only is there now a wide variety of media that can be accessed easily, but this media can be found in a wide variety of sources or created from scratch using an increasingly wide range of programs – see 'Multimodality' below. Whilst reading a big book with a class remains an important part of teaching, it is now possible to project large images of the page on to a screen using a visualiser, or a scan of the page on the IWB, to incorporate sound clips of children from the class reading it using digital recorders, with hyperlinks to pages on the Internet illustrating places from the story or an interview with the author on their own website. As will become apparent throughout this book, however, an effective teacher should not be seduced by all of the above into using ICT for the sake of it. It may be that reading children a big book is actually the most effective and appropriate strategy, and the ICT becomes an unnecessary distraction creating a barrier between teacher and pupils.

Provisionality

The key aspect of provisionality is the ability to explore ideas by asking the 'powerful question' (Loveless, 2003, p8): *what would happen if?* This question can, of course, be asked without using ICT. Indeed, the central part that dialogue plays in learning and teaching at all ages will be explored later. What we are considering here is how teachers and pupils can use the features of ICT to pose and investigate challenges, and explore concepts in a way that conventional resources (such as books) cannot.

CASE STUDY

A key stage 2 class are exploring different types of food as part of a balanced diet. The teacher has set up an Excel spreadsheet with relevant formulas linked from a variety of food groups to a variety of graph formats. This meant that as pupils entered information from tally sheets they had kept as food diaries, the associated graphs would change to reflect the information entered – see below. This spreadsheet was used in the first instance by the teacher on the IWB, but also later on PCs and laptops for individual and group workand to print out individual records.

On the IWB, the teacher was able to explore the impact of how changing the amount of different foods affected the graphs. As well as the real information entered, provisionality also allowed the class to explore how they could change the foods they ate to achieve a better balance and more healthy diet.

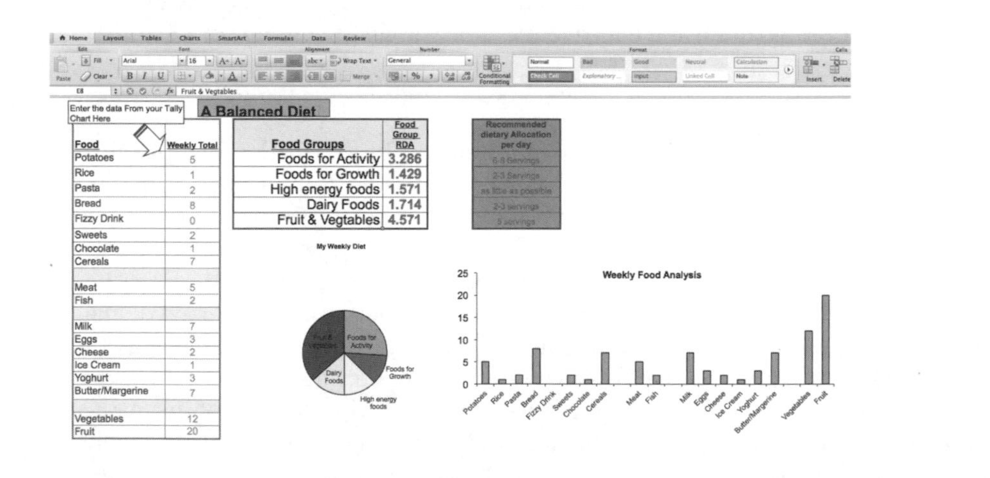

One way of posing 'what if' questions is to use undo and redo in many formats from text editing on PCs, through to maths work on the IWB. This ability to explore ideas could be considered an element of the beneficial 'playful' use of ICT, but can also lead to situations where pupils 'subvert' the learning intentions by adopting a trial and error approach to solving a problem. Such an approach can lead pupils to concentrate on the product (getting the right answer), rather than the process (the learning) (Beauchamp et al., 2010). It is worth considering whether pupils are adopting this approach whilst using ICT in tasks you set them. It can be easy to find out by just asking them what they are doing!

There is another facet of provisionality, which is important, and has a theme of trust. Such is the speed of advances in technology that even some students training to become teachers may not have been taught using blackboards, or possibly even wipe-clean whiteboards – but all will have used paper. Both blackboard and wipe-clean 'displays', and paper, make it almost impossible to totally erase what has gone before. In all of these examples, some visible evidence of a mistake will be left. On a computer, or IWB, this is not the case (although it does keep a non-visible trace which can be returned to) and it is possible to explore multiple ways of solving problems with no visible evidence of 'wrong' answers. Although this is perhaps more influential in pupil's work, it is also a consideration for teachers – but only if they operate an open classroom where mistakes are accepted as part of the learning process. In this context, the option for the teacher to be 'wrong' in front of the whole class, and to be prepared to explore other options openly, can send a powerful message to learners.

While we have seen above that there are negatives to provisionality, in general terms the provisional nature of ICT has many benefits, particularly when linked purposively to an interactive approach to learning.

Interactivity

The concept of interactivity in learning and teaching will be returned to in more detail later, but a brief overview of the concept is relevant at this stage. Although there is no agreed definition of what constitutes interactive teaching generally (Moyles et al., 2003), in our first encounter with the concept we can define it as ICT's ability to respond contingently (the response depending on the input, but limited to a pre-defined set of responses – unlike a teacher) in a variety of ways to input from different sources, both human and electronic. So, for instance, a pupil could input a number in a maths software package and the answer would be checked and summative feedback given, or a teacher could bring up a website on the interactive whiteboard and pupils could use it collaboratively to seek information on a topic. In addition, ICT can make such responses again and again without getting bored! Although this ability does allow pupils (or teachers) to practice new skills (such as addition or multiplication) repeatedly, it also allows them to make the same mistake every time as, unless it is programmed to do so, ICT resources are not really able to give a response which allows for personalised formative feedback. (See more on this in Chapter 3.)

Hargreaves et al., (2003, p224) classify interactivity into two broad forms. The first form contains classifications which are 'surface' forms of interactive teaching, which are 'associated by some teachers with "gimmicky" techniques such as the use of phoneme fans, various games or whiteboards'. The second form contains classifications which encourage a 'deeper level of engagement with the purposes of interactive teaching, to probe pupils' understanding, to try to ensure reciprocal interaction and the co-construction of meaning, or to enable children to consider or articulate their own thinking strategies'. These forms will be returned to in more detail in chapter two, but at this stage they draw attention to an important consideration for any ICT use: *am I using ICT (in any form) as a 'gimmick' (which will get attention or make my life easier) or as something which is essential to engage, challenge and develop thinking?*

In making these judgements, we should also note the useful distinction made by Smith et al., (2005) between *technical* interactivity (physical interaction with the device) and *pedagogic* interactivity (interaction between students and others in the classroom designed to bring about learning). Mercer et al., (2010, p197) define this as 'the distinction between what a piece of technology can do, and what it can be used to achieve educationally'. Although both are important, pedagogic rather than technical interactivity has currently been the focus of most research to date (Beauchamp et al., 2010) suggesting, as we have seen above, that it is not *what* is done with the technology but *why* and *how* it is done that is important.

Multimodal and multimedia capability

The multimodal capability of ICT is another reason to use it, as it allows teachers to present an idea in a variety of different ways to hep pupils understand it. It can also make work more interesting or motivating. Multimodal capability describes the facility of ICT to combine various modes (multimodal), such as visual, sounds and text, which are displayed through a variety of media (multimedia). Twiner et al., (2010, p212) summarise the distinction as mode being 'considered as the form of the content, such as image, writing or talk; while media refers to the vehicle through which information is conveyed, such as television, a book or website'. They also suggest that

> *the proliferation of new technologies has led to a culture permeated by multiple modes and media, in which communication is becoming increasingly more multimodal. … Increasing recognition of the pervasiveness of digital technologies and multimodal experiences in pupils' out-of-school lives therefore is exposing a need to incorporate such tools within teaching and learning, to enhance current and evolving pedagogic practice. (Twiner et al., 2010, p212)*

It could be argued that it has always been possible to present information in different modes using older media devices such as video, photographic slides, overhead projectors and so on. Indeed, all these resources do allow users to present ideas in a variety of ways, but when the modes are allied to the features of ICT above things can now be done quicker, from an ever expanding range of sources and in better quality. This is particularly true of the IWB. Hall and Higgins (2005, p106) found that the Year 6 pupils in their study seemed 'to enjoy in particular the multi-media capabilities of the technology, especially the visual aspects (colour and movement), audio (music, voice recordings, sound effects) and being able to touch the IWB. All pupil groups mentioned the multi-media aspects of the IWB as advantageous especially in engaging and holding their attention'.

This ability to engage and hold attention may also be enhanced by the ease with which pupils' own work can be used on the IWB. It is very easy to display and discuss word processing or picture files, pictures from digital cameras, movies from small movie cameras, readings from handheld data collectors, sound files of pupils themselves and so on. All of these help to make the work relevant and real to pupils of all ages. This is particularly true as such devices become smaller and easier to carry and use both indoors and out for younger children – and teachers!

Computer games in education

Another reason to use ICT, allied to advances in technology generally, but in multimodal capability in particular, is the use of computer games in education. In recent years, interest has grown considerably in the potential for play to form the basis for learning. This is especially true in the early years, with developments such as the Foundation Stage in England and the Foundation Phase in Wales. Using the features of ICT outlined above, technology can offer a specific type of play through computer or video games, which can be individual or whole class activities and may be particularly useful in Early Years teaching (Morgan, 2011). Interest in the potential for computer games in school is also influenced by the growing availability of computers in the home, but some research suggests that, despite parental aspirations for computers to be used educationally at home, children spend most of their time on games not found in schools (Kerawalla and Crook, 2002).

Research into the area of using computer games in education has tended to focus on two categories: firstly, the informal use of computer games outside educational settings (often called Commercial Off-The-Shelf Software [COTS]) and their potential for use in learning; and secondly, the use of games specifically developed for educational settings. Sandford and Williamson (2005, p1) suggest that games in the second category 'are designed to be as rich and dynamic as their mainstream "cousins", but are intended for particular formal educational outcomes'. The importance of teachers understanding this distinction is underlined by Sutherland et al., (2009, pp168–9) who draw attention to the potential for teachers and pupils to have 'radically different networks of meaning, resources and practices' when they refer to something as 'like a game'. This may be influenced by the fact that, at present (although this may change), although 85 per cent of children report they play computer games in their leisure time at least once fortnightly, only 28 per cent of teachers do. (Sandford et al., 2006) This has profound implications for teachers when they plan to use computer games in lessons. Not only do they have to become familiar with the games, they also have to ensure that they make clear the way in which they want for the game to be used. Sutherland et al., (2009, p169) give an example from a science lesson and suggest that

> *while the students, following the logic of domestic games play, are moving immediately into immersion – expecting to learn to rapid feedback on trial and error from the 'game' – the teacher is asking the students to step back, to reflect upon their decisions prior to starting activity, to carefully observe and document the implications of their choices – to learn from practices of scientific method.*

The same differing expectation could be possible in other areas of the curriculum and unclear expectations can lead to misunderstandings between teacher and pupil. It could be that the pupils who 'subverted' the activity in 'Provisionality' above, were in fact only adopting the normal practices they would use when playing a computer game, rather than trying to shortcut to find an answer.

Once common expectations are established, depending on the ICT resources available, and the learning intentions of the teacher, games can be played individually or in small groups on PCs, mobile devices or handheld gaming devices. They can be shared, if necessary, with the whole class or group, through the IWB, a data projector or television screen, or even between schools if web-based. Making decisions about how or if games are shared will be guided by the learning intention of the lesson – either academic or social. The type of skills that could be developed by ICT games are:

- strategic thinking
- planning
- communication
- application of numbers
- negotiating skills
- group decision-making
- data-handling

(Kirriemuir and McFarlane, 2004)

Obviously you need to be familiar with games to make decisions about which of these skills they can develop, if any. But while familiarity with games is important, Sandford et al., (2006, p3) suggest reassuringly that 'achieving particular educational objectives through the use of the game was more dependent upon a teacher's knowledge of the curriculum with which they were working than it was on their ability with the game'. Hence, perhaps more than any other area outlined in this chapter, the role of teacher in deciding on appropriate for use of games is important to ensure effective learning.

ACTIVITY

Think of a computer or web-based game you have used or seen in the classroom. In pairs or small groups, explain why you chose it and the strengths and weaknesses of it, with reference to a particular age group if necessary. Discuss if there are any common features that would help you to choose whether to use an ICT-based game in future teaching.

Mobility

In the early days of personal computers, users were forced to work at a fixed computer. Advances in technology now mean that computers can be taken to the work and increasingly other mobile devices, especially mobile phones and tablet-type PCs, have very advanced capabilities and can be used to supplement or even replace a laptop computer. This is an advantage with young children, as small devices are easy to carry. Such is the speed of change that by the time they leave primary school pupils may be able to do more things with a phone than they can with a computer. As we have seen above, the ability to work outside the classroom and carry work around with you is nothing new – a clipboard and a piece of paper can do the same thing. The advantage of using ICT is that the portability of work is complemented by the ability to produce high quality, collaborative and easily edited work, which can then be shared easily both through resources such as the IWB, or sent to other pupils or teachers both within the school grounds and beyond. Indeed, with the increasing use of networking and wireless technology (including Bluetooth) there is added scope for collaborating and communicating which will be discussed below.

Communication and collaboration

Having gathered a variety of information in a variety of forms, another feature of ICT which helps decide why we use it, is the ability to communicate this information with others and work collaboratively on it. The potential partners who can share information are not limited to the school as Virtual Learning Environments (VLEs), emails, texts and websites are increasingly being used to communicate with parents and other organisations. Again, there is nothing new in the ability to communicate, but what is different is how the features of ICT can be used to do this faster, using a variety of modes and media. The speed of communication is also important in developing interactivity, with responses often possible in real time allowing a meaningful dialogue to be carried out and lines of inquiry developed without delays interrupting the flow of thought. Developments in videoconferencing mean that it is possible to share not only text and speech in real time, but also to co-construct a range of materials, such as concept maps or designs, with instant feedback from collaborators – see more in Chapter 8. These collaborations can be between teachers and pupils, between pupils in pairs and groups and even between teachers. Again, there is nothing new in the idea of collaboration, but what is new is how ICT allows collaboration not only between those physically present, such as pupils anywhere in the school grounds within the school, but also between schools in the same country and even between schools across the world – but do you check your time zones (on your computer of course) before connecting!

Globalisation

The global reach facilitated by ICT allows pupils, individual classes and schools to have a global presence. This is not only restricted to the internet and school websites, but also through social networking and other media. There are obvious safety issues implicit in all sharing of information (see E-safety in Chapter 4),but the process for a school or nursery to make itself known around the world is now very straightforward. Besides the obvious promotional possibilities, there are also other benefits that can accrue. For teachers, one important benefit is that it is possible to build up online communities of settings who share similar practices. This may be particularly true of early years settings as practices such as the Foundation Phase in Wales (for children aged 3-7years), Forest Schools and other outdoor learning approaches become established. The possibility of teachers and pupils building communities of practice (Wenger, 1998),who share resources and advice is now very real and will be returned to in later chapters.

SUMMARY

This chapter has looked at why we should use ICT in learning and teaching in the primary school and identified a range of features of ICT which are available. We have begun to discuss the ownership and use of ICT resources and how control of this is evolving. In this evolution, however, even if pupils are actively involved in using ICT, and have well developed skills in using it, what they lack is a teacher's understanding of pedagogy that will enable effective learning to take place. Whilst it is important that teachers also maintain and develop their ICT skills, it is even more important that they develop their understanding of how to 'transform' knowledge (Shulman, 1987) using the features of ICT outlined above and when it is appropriate to do so. Hence, having established some of the many unique features of ICT and why we should use it, it is now necessary to examine how, when and who should use these features in the primary classroom and early years settings.

References

Beauchamp, G. and Kennewell, S. (2010), 'Interactivity in the classroom and its impact on learning', *Computers and Education,* 54, 759–66.

Beauchamp, G. , Kennewell, S., Tanner, H. and Jones, S. (2010), 'Interactive whiteboards and all that jazz: the contribution of musical metaphors to the analysis of classroom activity with interactive technologies', *Technology, Pedagogy and Education,* 19(2), 143–57.

DCSF (2009) *Independent Review of the Primary Curriculum: Final Report,* Annesley: DCSF.

Gillen, J., Littleton, K., Twiner, A., Staarman, J.K. and Mercer, N. (2008), 'Using the interactive whiteboard to resource continuity and support multimodal teaching in a primary science classroom', *Journal of Computer Assisted Learning,* 24, 348–58.

Hargreaves, L., Moyles, J., Merry, R., Paterson, F., Pell, A. and Esarte-Sarries, V. (2003), 'How do primary school teachers define and implement 'interactive teaching' in the National Literacy Strategy in England?', *Research Papers in Education,* 18:3, 217–36.

Hall, I. and Higgins, S. (2005), 'Primary school students' perceptions of interactive whiteboards', *Journal of Computer Assisted Learning,* 21, pp102–17.

Higgins, Steve (2001) 'ICT and Teaching for Understanding', *Evaluation and Research in Education,* 15: 3, 164–71.

Holmes, B. and Gardner, J.(2006), *E-learning: Concepts and Practice,* London: Sage Publications.

Kerawalla, L. and Crook, C. (2002), 'Children's computer use at home and at school: context and continuity', *British Educational Research Journal,* 28: 6, 751–71.

Kirriemuir, J and McFarlane, A. (2004), *Literature Review in Games and Learning,* Bristol: Futurelab.

Luckin, R. (2008). The learner centric ecology of resources: a framework for using technology to scaffold learning, *Computers and Education,* 50(2), 449–62.

Mayes, T. and de Freitas, S. (2007), 'Learning and e-learning: The role of theory' in Beetham, H. and Sharpe, R. (eds), *Rethinking Pedagogy for a Digital Age,* London: Routledge, pp13–25.

Mercer, N., Hennessy, S. and Warwick, P. (2010), 'Using interactive whiteboards to orchestrate classroom dialogue', *Technology, Pedagogy and Education,* 19: 2, 195–209.

Morgan, A. (2010), 'Interactive whiteboards, interactivity and play in the classroom with children aged three to seven years', *European Early Childhood Education Research Journal,* 18: 1, 93–104.

Sandford, R. and Williamson, B. (2005), *Games and Learning: A Handbook from Futurelab,* Bristol: Futurelab.

Sandford, R., Ulicsak, M., Facer, K. and Rudd, T. (2006), *Teaching with Games: Using Commercial Off-the-Shelf Computer Games in Formal Education,* Bristol: Futurelab.

Shulman, L.S. (1987). 'Knowledge and teaching: foundations of the new reform', *Harvard Educational Review,* 57(1), 1–22.

Tanner H., Jones S., Kennewell S. and Beauchamp G. (2005), 'Interactive whiteboards and pedagogies of whole class teaching', *Proceedings of MERGA28, Mathematics Education Research Group of Australasia Conference,* Melbourne, July 2005 [WWW Document.] URL **http://www.merga.net.au/documents/RP832005.pdf**

Twiner, A., Coffin, C., Littleton, K. and Whitelock, D. (2010), 'Multimodality, orchestration and participation in the context of classroom use of the interactive whiteboard: a discussion', *Technology, Pedagogy and Education,* 19: 2, 211–223.

Wertsch, J.V. (1991), *Voices of the Mind: A Sociocultural Approach to Mediated Action,* Hemel Hempstead, Harvester Wheatsheaf.

Further reading

Learning, Media and Technology 32(3), Special Issue: 'The interactive whiteboard phenomenon: reflections on teachers' and learners', responses to a novel classroom technology'.

Technology, Pedagogy and Education (2010), 19(2), Special Issue: 'Research into School Teaching and Learning with Whole Class Interactive Technologies'.

Sandford, R. and Williamson, B. (2005) Games and learning: A handbook from Futurelab, Bristol: Futurelab

ICT in the Primary Classroom: How, When and Who

In this chapter we will consider how, when and who should use ICT. We will consider the affordances of ICT and how they can contribute to personalised learning, interactive and dialogic teaching. Finally, we will consider how Shulman's model of pedagogical reasoning and action relates to ICT use in the primary classroom.

Let us begin this chapter by imagining the start of a lesson where you have carefully prepared an interactive whiteboard (IWB) activity where you guide the children through an example of drawing a graph. As you change variables, the graph changes in real time according to the input. A few minutes after you begin, a pupil puts up their hand and says 'but what about if you put a three there instead of a two'? This seemingly innocuous question actually poses a series of fundamental questions about the role of the teacher and learner, including who is in control of the learning and do pupils have a voice or role their own learning?

When responding to the question, you are faced with a number of options including:

- Ignore the child and carry on;
- put the new number there yourself and show the class what would happen;
- Ask the pupil to come to the IWB and explore what would happen for themselves;
- Ask the class what they think would happen and then invite someone to come and try.

The choice you make will depend on your pedagogical beliefs, your subject knowledge and understanding of the topic (with resultant confidence in dealing with unexpected questions) or, more pragmatically, if you are having a good or bad day! Assuming you are able to rise above a bad day, and having made the decision (why) to use ICT in the first place, by choosing your course of action you are beginning to address *how, when* and *who* should use ICT.

In order to help in making these decisions it is useful to consider the different roles that ICT can play, which will help in allocating these roles to different actors (people in the classroom). I have suggested elsewhere (Beauchamp, 2011) that a useful categorisation might be:

Category of use	End product
a. A ***passive* tool** for interactions: ICT provides structure and capability to complete a **teacher** directed task (such as 'writing up') or **teacher** demonstration / modelling	• teacher-led demonstration (normally to whole class) or modelling of task with some limited opportunities for pupils to clarify with teacher control of ICT • minimal dialogue/ discussion about nature of task
b. The ***object*** of interaction: resources to interact ***about*** (e.g. video clip or pupil's work) where the ***teacher*** usually provides the structure for interactions	• dialogue / discussion about content of lesson
c. A **participant** in interaction: a partner to interact ***with*** when ***ICT*** sets tasks and provides immediate feedback (such as a game, quiz or simulation)	• completed task / discussion to complete task if more than one person
d. An ***active* tool** for interaction: a medium to interact **through** (e.g. email/chat, annotation, mind-mapping) where **learners** usually provide the structure for interactions	• dialogue / discussion / learning / co-construction of knowledge

In the example above, you could choose between most of these categories or none of the options. In making this choice, you are making a fundamental decision about the locus of control in the classroom and hence who has power over of the direction of learning, you or the pupil? In the split second in which you make this choice, it is very unlikely you will consciously use the categorisation above, but if you are aware of it, it may influence you subconsciously – or at least cross your mind when you evaluate the lesson and consider what you could have done differently. One of the main purposes of this book is to bring to your attention a wide range of pedagogic ideas relating to ICT, all informed by research and classroom experience. You may use some ideas in this 'pedagogic toolkit' more than others, but the key idea to that you have the tools and know how to use them and what they do. At the same time you will be developing practical skills in, and knowledge of, how particular hardware or software works. As programs evolve, you will need to keep updating these practical skills, but you will also need to do the same thing for your ICT pedagogic skills. At times one can inform, or trigger, the other. In some research projects I have undertaken with primary teachers, showing them a new facet of a program results in an immediate recognition of how it could work in a lesson: 'Oh, I didn't know you would do that but I could use it for …'.

Conole and Dyke (2004, pp114–15) suggest that

> *We believe that a better understanding of the nature and properties of technologies will lead to a more systematic application of the use of ICT for learning and teaching. … evidence suggests that practitioners are still unclear about how to use technology appropriately, and its application is often based on common sense rather then being theoretically informed by pedagogical theory.*

To encourage greater use of research informed pedagogic theory ('I am doing this because I have researched it and several researchers, using sound methods, have found that it is effective'), rather than 'common sense' ('I am doing this because it seems the obvious/easiest thing to do and I haven't got much time'), this chapter will examine a range of ideas which influence ICT pedagogy.

Affordances

The first of these relates to seeing the possibilities that ICT can offer to both teacher and pupils. The idea of 'affordance' is normally attributed to Gibson (1979) in the first instance, but has been used by many others since in many areas of the curriculum (for example, Kennewell, 2001; Conole and Dyke, 2004; John and Sutherland, 2005, Webb, 2005; Warwick and Kershner, 2008). Essentially, an affordance 'refers to the perceived and actual properties of a thing, primarily those functional properties that determine just how the thing could possibly be used'. (Pea, 1993, p51) Alternatively, Kennewell (2001, p106) suggests that affordances are the 'attributes of the setting which provide potential for action'. As such, affordances can be considered as preconditions for activity, but, even though they are there, this does not mean that activity will take place, as the affordances need to be perceived by, in our context, the learner or teacher. As Hammond (2010, p206) points out, 'the affordance is there, it has always has been there, but it needs to be perceived to be realised. ... The world is full of potential, not of things'.

One example could be the handle on a door, which has many affordances – although perhaps with little educational value beyond allowing access to the classroom. For instance, you could hang your coat on it, or even tie a skipping rope on it and have a tug of war with the door! In reality, the two main affordances are opening and shutting the door. In the same way, ICT hardware and software have many affordances and pupils are not afraid to 'play' to find these out – see more later in this book. The role of the teacher in this context is to be sure that the most suitable (educational) affordances of all resources (especially in this context of ICT) are identified and used, but also to provide the opportunity for pupils to see and use others. In doing this, however, you will need to be aware that affordances are not the same for everyone and different affordances can be seen by different people – some of your pupils might enjoy the challenge of door tug of war and see it as an obvious thing to do with the door handle!

Considering the affordances of ICT (both in terms of hardware and software) can also be useful in many ways, particularly in taking into consideration how you are going to differentiate activities for different pupils or in different subjects – again, more on the latter to come in later chapters. You will need to take account of several factors as the affordances for each may vary. These could include the age of the pupils, their level of maturity / independence, any special needs, or their knowledge of how to use a particular piece of soft/hardware.

ACTIVITY

Consider a piece of software that you know well and identify the affordances it offers and how they could be used with a class you teach or are familiar with.

Person-plus – distributed cognition

The affordances outlined above form part of the surroundings in the classroom and are resources to be used. The importance of using these surroundings is stressed by Perkins (1993, p89), who makes the distinction between the *person-solo*, "the person without resources in his or her surround" and the *person-plus*, "the person plus [their] surround". This theory suggests that 'thinking and learning for the person-plus depend only on what might be called the "access characteristics" of relevant knowledge – what kind of knowledge is represented, how it is represented, how readily it is retrieved, and related matters – and not whether the knowledge is located in the person or the surround'. The question posed to support this suggestion is, if a pupil can access information about a specific thing from a notebook 'because they have organised it so well, does it really matter whether the ideas lie inside or outside the student's cranium?'. (Perkins, 1993, p90) It is easy to see that ICT in many forms could replace the notebook in this example.

This framework is intended to help achieve an 'information flow analysis' in a person-plus situation where thinking and learning are distributed between the pupil and their surroundings. The learner picks up information from various points in the system and uses it. The four components of the framework are discussed below.

Knowledge

For teachers, this involves factual and procedural knowledge, including knowledge of ICT hardware and software, as well as higher-order knowledge, such as problem-solving strategies, explanation and knowledge and understanding of pedagogy. In this context, it is likely that the teacher has much of the higher-order knowledge and not the pupils or the surroundings. The *teacher-solo* would have a 'rich technical repertoire' (of teaching) in long term memory, but the teacher also needs more, the 'plus' provided by things likes books, videos, ICT and indeed the pupils themselves.

Representation

This relates to how the knowledge is represented, in particular, in ways that make it easily picked up, transported in the system, and recoded. In terms of ICT, this could be how ICT allows you to represent models of complex subjects, which Perkins suggests is of most benefit to 'less able learners'. The *teacher-solo* will have mental images, but the *teacher-plus* has other ways of representing and exploring ideas – in which multimedia and multimodality may be particularly useful. This can range from pen and paper to using features and range of ICT. (See also use 'Representation' below, p23)

Retrieval

Retrieval concerns whether the system can find the knowledge representations in question, and how efficiently. Perkins contends that knowledge can exist in a system but may not have suitable 'retrieval characteristics' for it to be used effectively. Besides conventional ways of retrieving information from books, ICT allows quick and easy retrieval of information from a range of resources such as CD-ROMs, searchable databases and websites and, increasingly commonly, internet search engines such as Google – although with these searches there are resultant issues of literacy to which we will return to in Chapter 7.

Construction

This relates to the (knowledge processing) system's capacity to assemble the pieces of knowledge retrieved into new knowledge structures. Perkins draws attention to the importance of this in view of problems caused by limitations in short memory, which make some concepts inaccessible to learners. It is suggested that a well-designed surround, including ICT, can provide a 'surrogate short-term memory' to support learners in mastering these concepts.

Perkins suggests that it should be possible for pupils to make better use of the cognitive resources around them to make their own 'personal plus', including their use of ICT resources, which would accord with theories of child-centred learning examined elsewhere in this book. The key message about the best use of ICT in the person-plus model is that it should allow learners to do more than they can do alone or with other non-ICT resources in the classroom.

Interactive teaching

The interactions with others and the surroundings form the basis of the concept of interactivity. In chapter 1 we began to consider the notion of teaching as a socio-cultural activity, where actions are mediated by tools (including ICT), the most important of which is language. Nevertheless, the features of the setting and the pedagogic beliefs of teachers play an important role. The features of the setting can include physical (the classroom itself and equipment within it), human (everybody in the classroom) and intellectual (the belief systems of the people). The pedagogic beliefs of the teacher will play an important role in deciding how to these factors are used and by whom. Traditionally, the teacher will organise, or orchestrate, the features of the setting. The idea of orchestration is set in a socio-cultural perspective on activity where, as we saw in chapter 1, people and objects interact and provide the context for the activity. Beauchamp and Kennewell (2010, p760) suggest

> *The people involved will include teachers, support staff, and students; objects commonly employed include books, pens, stories, ICT resources. Orchestration is a conscious and contingent arrangement, dynamic re-arrangement, and emphasis of these elements and their affordances in order to facilitate the achievement of goals. It may be carried out by the teacher, the students, or even ICT resources, often in combination.*

One aspect of this orchestration of resources is based on beliefs about interactivity. Interactive teaching is a commonly used phrase and has been advocated widely in official policy documents. Despite this extensive use, it is very difficult to find an actual definition of the term in these documents. In the academic literature there *have* been many attempts to define interactive teaching, but a commonly accepted definition still remains elusive. This situation is complicated due to the many different types of interactivity that are possible within whole class, group and individual work, especially in the primary classroom. What does emerge from the literature are attempts to characterise the features of interactive lessons. Burns and Myhill (2004) suggest the following characteristics:

- Reciprocal opportunities for talk which allow children to develop independent voices in discussion;
- Appropriate guidance and modeling when the teacher orchestrates (organises) the language and skills for thinking collectively;
- Environments which are conducive to student participation;
- An increase in the level of student autonomy.

In lessons which display these characteristics, Hargeaves et al., (2003) suggest it is possible to identify different levels of interactivity, which may be broadly classified into two groups:

- 'Surface' interactivity: engaging pupils, practical and active involvement/participation, collaborative activity, emphasising recall, conveying knowledge
- 'Deep' interactivity: assessing and extending knowledge, emphasising understanding, attention to thinking and learning skills (Hargreaves et al., 2003)

As we have seen above, ICT can contribute to both of these levels of interactivity, from engaging pupils with a new, but not necessarily challenging, feature of the technology (such as writing your name in smiley faces with your finger on the IWB), (surface), through to posing cognitively challenging activities designed to focus attention on thinking and learning skills (deep). It is suggested that most meaningful teaching at all ages should aim to move beyond surface to deep interactivity. One way of doing this is to combine effective talk with the use of ICT.

Dialogic teaching with ICT

We have already seen above that language remains the most important tool in the classroom context. Alexander (2008, pp37–8) makes a compelling case for raising further the profile of talk in the classroom, but argues

> *not for more of the same kind of classroom talk that children already encounter, but for a particular kind of interactive experience which we call dialogic teaching. Dialogic teaching harnesses the power of talk to engage children, stimulate and extend their thinking, and advance their learning and understanding. Not all classroom talk secures these outcomes, and some may even discourage them.*

He goes on to outline five most important principles of dialogic teaching and there are obvious overlaps with the features of interactive teaching already outlined above. Dialogic teaching is:

- *Collective* – teachers and pupils work together;
- *Reciprocal* – teachers and pupils listen to each other, share ideas and discuss different viewpoints;
- *Supportive* – pupils speak freely, are not afraid of 'wrong' answers, and help each other to develop common understandings;

- *Cumulative* – teachers and pupils build on each other's ideas and develop them into clear lines of thinking and enquiry;
- *Purposeful* – teachers plan for and steer classroom talk with specific educational goals in view.

WHAT DO YOU THINK?

Consider a recent lesson you have seen or been part of and decide if this could be described as dialogic teaching. As you think about it, also consider what role, if any, did ICT play? *If it was dialogic, what did the teacher do to make it so; if it was not, what needed to be done to make it dialogic?*

In making decisions about what constitutes dialogic teaching, it can be useful to contrast it with an 'authoritative' approach (Scott et al., 2006) – in which the views of the teacher dominate – and with dialectic' teaching – with an emphasis on overcoming disparities between students' thinking and formal knowledge (Wegerif, 2008). Beauchamp and Kennewell (2010, p760) suggest that "effective teaching, however, is likely to demonstrate a variety of these characteristics in an appropriate combination; in particular, there is an important interplay between dialogic and dialectic forms of interaction, although the relative importance of each will depend on what is to be learned (Ravenscroft, Wegerif, and Hartley, 2007)".

From this viewpoint, and the range of possible approaches considered above, we have now arrived at a point where we consider in more detail how to transform them into tangible outcomes in the classroom, using ICT as appropriate. In the remainder of this chapter, we will examine how ICT can develop deep interactivity in the context of Shulman's model of pedagogic reasoning, as well as how it can be used in the context of dialogic and dialectic teaching in the primary classroom or early years setting. We will continue to adopt a generic perspective and will not yet consider in detail the potential impact of subject or age specific (especially the early years) pedagogy, but this will be considered in later chapters. In doing so, we will in part be fulfilling the requirements for student teachers to have a knowledge and understanding of a range of teaching and learning strategies and know how to use and adapt them. We will also, however, be moving beyond knowledge and understanding to developing a critically evaluative mindset which can be applied at all stages of a teacher's career.

Pedagogic reasoning and ICT in the primary classroom

The cycle of planning, teaching, assessing and evaluating is familiar to all teachers. In 1987, Shulman proposed a model of pedagogical reasoning and action which outlined the knowledge needed during this cycle:

- Comprehension
- Transformation

- Instruction
- Evaluation
- Reflection
- New comprehensions

In each of these categories there is a role for ICT, from your use of the internet to help your own comprehension, to providing affordances to help you to transform what you have to teach, to providing many possible ways (multimodal and multimedia) to represent ideas or present analogies, and even helping you record evaluation of lessons. The decision to use ICT, however, and the sophistication of its use, can range from very simple to very complex depending on the age and ability of the class and your own ability to recognise the unique contribution that ICT can make. We will consider each stage of Shulman's model of pedagogic reasoning in more detail and suggest how ICT can contribute to each.

Comprehension

The first stage is comprehension and is defined as comprehension of

- purposes
- subject matter structures
- ideas within and outside the discipline

From this list it becomes apparent that it is not just understanding the subject, but as Shulman (1987, p15) states 'the key to distinguishing the knowledge base of teaching lies at the intersection of content and pedagogy, and the capacity of a teacher to transform the content knowledge he or she possesses into forms that are pedagogically powerful and yet adaptive to the variations in ability of background presented by the students'. Shulman makes it clear that teachers should understand what they teach and when possible, to understand it in different ways, not only to reinforce comprehension but also to allow them to think of different forms of representation later in the process. In the primary and early years classroom / setting, it is also important to consider how your understanding, or comprehension, in one area of learning or subject can be integrated into and reinforce other areas. Although guidance is given by many official sources, and many books offer 'subject knowledge', there is still some freedom for teachers to develop their own understanding and how it can apply in the primary classroom. Having said this, the role of ICT in comprehension is perhaps rather limited, although it can have a role in developing your subject knowledge, especially the use of internet sources – although, as with its use with pupils, you need to be selective to ensure you get information (and hence understanding) which is accurate.

Transformation

The next stage in the process is transforming your understanding into a form that can be understood by your pupils. Perhaps more than any other part of the process, the features and capabilities of ICT which we looked at in chapter one offer unique ways of transforming and representing ideas. Shulman (1987, p16) suggests that transformations 'require some combination or ordering' of the following processes:

- *Preparation*
- *Representation*
- *Selection*
- *Adaptation and tailoring to student characteristics*

It is important to note that these processes may not all be needed and should not be considered as sequential. As we have seen before, the teacher remains central to the success of using this model. It is the teacher who decides what will be combined with what and how this will be ordered, not the ICT. ICT can help mechanically in the process, but it cannot help with pedagogic decisions. You need to apply your own professional judgment when selecting from your curricular and ICT 'repertoire', which will increase throughout your career. This will apply particularly in 'preparation', where you consider how you can structure and segment your understanding into a suitable sequence of ideas as you transform your understanding of one 'big' idea into a series of smaller ones that can be understood by pupils. In this you will be guided by your knowledge of how the features of ICT can effectively represent or demonstrate your analogies or examples. You will also consider how ICT can help you organise and manage your teaching. In addition, you will also need to reflect on how ICT can then be used, or not used, to meet the needs of your pupils. From this, it becomes obvious that there is not a logical sequence to be followed as it may be that a particular feature of ICT (for example, automation) triggers an idea about how to represent an idea, which will in turn guide how you organise your lesson. Or, it could be that the needs of your pupils have to guide all other considerations. We will consider each process in more detail to establish how ICT can help.

Preparation

- Critical interpretation and analysis of 'texts', structuring and segmenting, development of a curricular repertoire, and clarification of purposes.

The word 'text' in this context can be considered as your starting point for the teaching activity. It could literally be a written text or could take any other form of material or idea that you need to interpret critically and/or analyse to use in teaching. Although researching with ICT can help in this, perhaps its most relevant use in this stage is in helping to structure and segment ideas. This feature is inherent in presentation programs such as PowerPoint which, although perhaps a more functional use of ICT, forces you to consider the structure and sequence of ideas (using, for example, the 'slide sorter' view) as you organise and reorganise segments of a lesson or even a sequence of lessons. An important part of this process is deciding when you are going to leave the 'presentation' facility of ICT to make best use of another feature or decide not use ICT at all, for example to undertake a practical activity. In addition, it is important to plan opportunities for talk and other interactions to develop dialogic and interactive lessons.

Representation

- Use of a representational repertoire which includes analogies, metaphors, examples, demonstrations, explanations, and so forth.

A particular strength of ICT in this process is that it can meet Shulman's contention (p16) that 'multiple forms of representation are desirable'. In Chapter 1 we discussed the potential of the multimedia and multimodal capabilities of ICT and this is one area where they may be very useful. However, just because ICT *can* do this, it does not mean that it *should* be used. The main questions are:

1. Do the features of ICT allow it to provide representations (e.g. analogies, metaphors or examples) well and/or in a better way than any other resources?
2. Will this work for *my class* (with my ICT resources)?

The importance of the second question will be returned to in 'adaptation and tailoring' below, but the first question is perhaps most important. By considering each to the features of ICT (see Chapter 1) you can decide if one, or a combination of them, makes ICT the best choice of tool / medium to transform and organise your understanding into something meaningful for your class. The caveat for this is that just using ICT will not be enough on its own and it will remain just part of your repertoire of teaching to be used in conjunction with other resources in a dialogic or interactive context.

Selection

Consideration of the use of ICT is part of the 'selection', which Shulman suggests is making a choice from among an 'instructional repertoire', which includes modes of teaching, organising, managing, and arranging. The ability to do this will depend of your level of experience and will continue to evolve at all stages of your career. Modes of teaching could include whole class and other types of grouping. Again, we will need to consider the best use of ICT within each of these these contexts. For instance, much research has been done which shows the IWB can be very effective in whole class teaching (for example, Somekh et al., 2007), but it may be more appropriate to use laptops or tablet PCs in group work – although there is no reason the IWB cannot be a group activity on its own as part of a 'circus' of activities. In addition, you may be more confident in certain types of class organisation at different points in your training or career, which may be reflected in your ability to select from a 'repertoire' and your confidence in doing so.

Adaptation and tailoring to student characteristics

- Consideration of conceptions, preconceptions, misconceptions, and difficulties, language, culture, and motivations, social class, gender, age, ability, aptitude, interests, self-concepts, and attention.

When making a 'selection', it is necessary to take account of the needs of your pupils. Although all teachers need high expectations of *all* pupils, it is important to acknowledge that not every group of learners is the same, as shown by the fact that teachers need to differentiate work in all lessons, even if doing the same lesson for two classes of the same age. Although there is a pragmatic use of ICT in accessing records of prior work and checking previous achievements (for example, difficulties and misconceptions), 'adaptation and tailoring' work to pupils perhaps makes less use of ICT than other parts of this model of teaching, although it remains central to effective lessons. As many of the features of adaptation and tailoring above are covered in great detail in more generic teaching texts, and as we will be examining the impact of a pupil's age later in this book, we will consider here the potential impact of adapting and tailoring the ICT resources you have available.

The first consideration, already mentioned above, is who is in control of the ICT? If the pupils are used to making use of ICT as an active tool to interact through (see Beauchamp 2011 table above) you can tailor your use of ICT to this. If they are not used to this approach, you need to adapt ICT use (by you and the pupils) accordingly. In addition, you need to tailor your use of ICT to the relevant skills that you and your pupils possess in different areas of the curriculum. This can range from knowledge of the affordances of a particular piece of software through to how to manipulate a particular piece of hardware, such as the IWB or visualiser. It is worth mentioning here that you also need to adapt your work to the version of the software used by the school if relevant. It is very frustrating when you have used a newer version of software to develop ICT work at home, only to realise that the school uses an older version of the software which will not open your files – especially if you are a student teacher and your tutor (or external examiner), or inspector, is watching you!

ACTIVITY

In groups, or on your own, decide on a topic, idea or concept that you are going to teach. Identify the 'big ideas' in this and organise these into the sequence they need to be taught to ensure sound understanding. Next, thinking of a class you are familiar with, break down each 'big' idea into smaller ideas that will need to be taught as part of this idea. Continue this process as necessary and then decide which of these can be taught as they stand and which will need to be 'transformed'. When these ideas are identified split into those that will use the features of ICT well, and those are better done using other resources. Finally, decide how you will use ICT for some or all of the ideas.

Presentation packages, such as PowerPoint, can be useful for sequencing ideas. You can add slides for smaller ideas and also use the 'Slide sorter' view to see the flow of ideas and to reorganise as appropriate.

Instruction

- Management, presentations, interactions, group work, discipline, humour, questioning, and other aspects of active teaching, discovery or inquiry instruction, and the observable forms of classroom teaching

When you reach the instruction stage you have moved beyond the planning stage (which can take place anywhere) to actually being with a class of children ready to begin a lesson. You will already have checked that all the hardware and software is compatible and functioning, all the pupils are there and you are ready to start your lesson. Although there are lots of pedagogic issues to be considered in the 'instruction' phase, many of them are related to generic classroom management. As above, these are covered in many existing texts on classroom teaching, so we will concentrate on how ICT can be used effectively in this context in a generic sense – we will consider use in different subjects and areas of learning in later chapters.

We have already considered different types of interactions so let us first consider management and presentation. ICT does provide a good tool to manage and organise your lesson content through a variety of software. ICT also provides a wide range of media to present or share your lesson content, such as computers or visualisers, through a wide variety of modes, such as movies or sound files. ICT also allows you the opportunity to use humour (an unexpected effect, image or movie clip / sound file) and pose questions or stimulate debate through unusual images. This can take many forms and is not always restricted by the limitations of a program if you are prepared to try new ideas and consider how the features of ICT can be used effectively or creatively.

CASE STUDY

PowerPoint has many limitations, and is ultimately a presentation program, but one teacher used it to show her class two contrasting automated slide shows of images, both accompanied by the Louis Armstrong song, 'What a wonderful world'. The first showed some of the wonders of the world such as the diversity of life in a rain forest, pyramids, waterfalls and so on; the second with the same song in the background was of devastated rain forests, polluted seas, war zones and so on. The rest of the lesson concentrated on the discussion of the content. ICT has served its purpose, to do something it was good at, and was not used again.

Evaluation

- Checking for student understanding during interactive teaching
- Testing student understanding of the end of lessons or units

ICT tools in general are not good at helping you to reflect on your lessons; except, perhaps, video recordings of lessons used on some training courses. What it can do is provide one quick way of testing pupils' understanding through the use of tests or other activities and of keeping a record of outcomes. The limitation of this is ICT's inability to provide formative feedback beyond pre-programmed responses. Again, you need to make decisions about why you are using ICT and decide if it serves a purpose to advance learning?

Evaluating one's own performance, and adjusting for experiences: Reflection and New Comprehensions

In addition to evaluating the outcome of the lesson for the pupils we also need to evaluate our own performance as a teacher. As above, video recording lessons can be useful and ICT can help you to record your thoughts and your new understanding, but in reality is possibly less useful here than other parts of this process.

SUMMARY

In this chapter we have considered how, when and who should use ICT. We have examined the concepts of interactive and dialogic teaching and how ICT can allow both teachers and learners to become active partners (co-constructors of knowledge) in the learning process. We have also considered some of the strengths of ICT in relation to Shulman's model and the different roles it can play in the classroom for both teachers and pupils. As the role of the teacher changes to facilitate greater pupil autonomy (at all ages), the next chapter will consider how this be developed in the context of the primary classroom.

References

Beauchamp, G. (2011), Interactivity and ICT in the primary school: categories of learner interactions with and without ICT, *Technology, Pedagogy and Education,* 20(2), 175–90.

Conole, G. and Dyke, M. (2004), 'What are the affordances of information and communication technologies?', *ALT-J,* 12(2), 113–24.

Hammond, M. (2010), 'What is an affordance and can it help us understand the use of ICT in education?', *Education and Information Technology,* 15(3), 205–17.

John, P. and Sutherland, R. (2005), 'Affordance, opportunity and the pedagogical implications of ICT', *Educational Review,* 57(4), 405–13.

Pea, R.D. (1997) 'Distributed intelligence and designs for education', in Salomon, G. (ed.), *Distributed Cognitions: Psychological and Educational Considerations,* Cambridge: Cambridge University Press, pp. 47–87.

Perkins, D. N. (1997). 'Person-plus: a distributed view of thinking and learning', in Salomon, G. (ed.), *Distributed Cognitions: Psychological and Educational Considerations,* Cambridge: Cambridge University Press, 88–110.

Ravenscroft, A., Wegerif, R., and Hartley, R. (2007).' Reclaiming thinking: dialectic, dialogic and learning in the digital age', in Underwood, J. and Dockrell, J. (eds), *Learning through Digital Technologies,* London: British Psychological Society.

Scott, P. H., Mortimer, E. F., and Aguiar, O. G. (2006), 'The tension between authoritative and dialogic discourse: a fundamental characteristic of meaning making interactions in high school science lessons', *Science Education,* 90, 605–31.

Shulman, L. S. (1987) 'Knowledge and teaching: Foundations of the new reform', *Harvard Educational Review,* Feb. 1987: 1–22.

Somekh, B. and Davies, R. (1991) 'Towards a pedagogy for information technology', *The Curriculum Journal,* 2, pp. 153–70.

Somekh, B., Haldane, M., Jones, K., Lewin, C., Steadman, S., Scrimshaw, P., Sing, S., Bird, K., Cummings, J., Downing, B., Harber Stuart, T., Jarvis, J., Mavers, D. and Woodrow, D. (2007), 'Evaluation of the Primary Schools Whiteboard Expansion Project – summary report', Manchester Metropolitan University: Centre for ICT, Pedagogy and Learning.

Webb, M. (2005) 'Affordances of ICT in science learning: implications for an integrated pedagogy', *International Journal of Science Education,* 27(6), 705–35.

Wegerif, R. (2008). 'Dialogic or dialectic? The significance of ontological assumptions in research on educational dialogue', *British Educational Research Journal,* 34(3), 347–61.

Further reading

Alexander, R. (2008), *Dialogic teaching,* 4th edition, York: Dialogos.

Beauchamp, G. and Kennewell, S. (2010), 'Interactivity in the classroom and its impact on learning', *Computers and Education,* 54, 759–66.

Shulman, L. S. (1987) 'Knowledge and teaching: foundations of the new reform', *Harvard Educational Review,* Feb. 1987: 1–22.

CHAPTER 3 ICT and the Child: Theories of Learning

In this chapter we will focus on learners and how they learn. After a brief examination of **why** children need to learn, we will continue to examine a range of learning theories and relate them to the role and purpose of ICT.

So far we have discussed theories of ICT pedagogy, but we now need to explore how these are based upon, and try to develop, more generic theoretical perspectives on how children learn. This process is not straightforward as these perspectives are informed by, and situated in, complex and contested views of the nature and purpose of education itself. Bartlett and Burton (2007, p11) sum up the views of many when they suggest that 'the meaning of the term "education" and its purpose is not universally fixed and is not the same for all of us'. They suggest it is shaped by factors including individual experiences and a range of beliefs and values. Perhaps the most important of all in terms of their impact are the beliefs and values of decision makers (including leaders at both national and local levels) and their resultant vision of the role of ICT in education. As such, although there is not space to explore all relevant issues in depth, it is necessary to consider briefly the role and purpose of education in its widest sense and how ICT may fit within it to see how these views may be formed.

What is education for and what is the role of ICT within it?

We can begin by acknowledging that there exist many different, and sometimes irreconcilable, ideologies of education which emphasise different targets such as:

- **The individual** – an emphasis on individual development based on the needs of the learner;
- **Formal knowledge** for its own sake – either in subjects or a less prescribed format;
- **Society** – the importance of education to the economy or to democratising or reshaping society.

There is a role for ICT in all of these systems and sometimes it can even influence the direction of education. As Kelly (2009, p5) points out when considering the major changes in education in recent years, it is not surprising that

> *the nature and structure of our education system should have been changing so extensively at a time when we have been experiencing social change of an equally dramatic kind, much of it prompted by a rapid technological advance. ... the education system is a social institution which should be expected to change along with other such institutions.*

One rather extreme view of the impact of ICT, or more specifically computers, was offered in the late 1970s by the influential writer Seymour Papert (1993, p9) when he suggested that 'schools as we know them today will have no place in the future. But it is an open question whether they will adapt by transforming themselves into something new or wither away and be replaced'. One of the premises of this book is that ICT will allow teachers and pupils to transform schools into something new with the creative and imaginative use of ICT. Many of the ideas discussed, however, apply just as well to the use of ICT within a virtual environment, with no physical structure or location which pupils attend. Indeed, many primary schools increasingly use new technologies to transform the classroom *and* use Virtual Learning Environments (VLEs) to provide both a real and a virtual approach to schooling, hence resolving Papert's dichotomy above.

Other less radical views of the importance and role of ICT reflect the educational ideologies discussed above and are summarised in Table 3.1 below.

Table 3.1 Three purposes of education

Individual	**Formal learning**	**Society**
ICT provides the means to: • increase attainment and/or achievement through personalised learning • enhance access, especially for those with Special Educational Needs (SEN) • provide access to remote learners, teachers and content	• ICT provides access to a large body of knowledge with information available directly from primary sources – and some less reputable! • This information can be retrieved quickly and in a variety of formats	Children need to learn ICT skills: • as necessity for economic competitiveness in a knowledge society • as preparation for the world of work • to access information and learning which allows children of all backgrounds to develop and succeed • to develop greater economic activity in the longer term though increased e-commerce

Source: OECD, 2001.

What is immediately apparent from this table is that primary schools have a role to play in all of these categories. What is also apparent is that some areas would be addressed by the curriculum and others by extra-curricular activities. Even within the curriculum, some areas, such as I(C)T skills, may be specific to one subject in the first instance, but then applied across different areas of learning or subjects – see more later.

If we accept that, whatever justification is adopted, children will need to be educated, we now need to consider how they will actually learn and how ICT can contribute. We need to be aware, however, that even theories of learning can be subject to the same ideological influences. This does not make them less valuable, and whilst the advocacy of a particular theory examined below may be based on ideological influences at a meta-level (such as the government), or at a micro-level (such as an individual teacher in the classroom), decisions are made to use many, or even all, theories based on the needs of individual children.

ICT and how children learn: learning theory and learners

What is learning?

As with trying to define the purpose and nature of education, it is difficult to come up with an agreed definition of learning. Therefore, it is perhaps best to work with a broad conception of what happens when someone learns something. Woolfolk et al., (2008, p244) suggest that, broadly speaking, learning occurs when 'experience causes a relatively permanent change in an individual's knowledge or behavior.' They suggest that these changes are not the result of maturation and propose that temporary changes caused by, for example, illness or fatigue, should be excluded (as you do not learn to be hungry just because you do not have food). This definition, however, highlights one of the essential difficulties with studying learning in that we can *see* changes in behavior, but it is much harder to assess what someone knows or understands – particularly when they make not be able to express themselves clearly due to maturational, linguistic or other factors. As Meadows (2004, p142) points out, 'we do not directly observe thinking or other cognitive processes, we infer them from observable behavior'. Nevertheless, it is this emphasis on observable behavioursthat brings us to the first of our learning theories: behaviourism.

Behaviourism

Although dating from the Enlightenment period, behaviourism is a 'philosophy, theory and pedagogy' which was a 'strong force' in education from early in the twentieth century until the mid-1970s. (Woollard, 2010, pp1–2) It is predicated on the idea that all behaviours are the result of conditioning, caused by interactions with the environment. Behaviourists suggest that if the resultant behaviours are observed in a systematic way there is no need to consider consciousness or internal states. Although we necessarily need to summarise the key ideas of behaviourism, to see how this theory can be applied to ICT in education we do need to consider the distinction between the two major types of conditioning: classical and operant, or instrumental, conditioning.

Classical conditioning

In classical conditioning the key idea is the linking of stimulus and response. The most famous example, and the foundation for much that followed, was the work of Pavlov (1927) who found that dogs could be taught to salivate at a given signal that food was about to arrive. The response was not to the unconditioned stimulus provided by the food, but to the conditioned stimulus (to the signal, such as a buzzer) and 'when the response is elicited only from the conditioned stimulus, it is regarded as a conditioned response.' (Jarvis et al., 2003, p27) These ideas were extended to humans by Watson (1925). For our purposes, we need to understand that although some dispute if this approach results in learning, as it is simply reflexive, it can have an impact in some situations – such as liking a subject in school because you like the teacher – or one might even suggest, a piece of technology!

Operant conditioning

In operant conditioning the central idea, originating from the work of Skinner (1938), is the linking of reward and punishment with behavior, resulting in an association between a type of behaviour and the consequence of it. The name derives from the idea that a person can act, or operate, on their environment to attain the outcome they desire. There are three components to this process: the antecedents (what comes before), the behaviour and the consequences (Yeomans and Arnold, 2006). The consequences (such as the reaction of a teacher or indeed a computer) can encourage or discourage and are labelled reinforcers or punishers accordingly. In classroom terms, and for the purposes of how these ideas apply to ICT, this may simply be regarded as praise or punishment – the latter being interpreted as many approaches, such as sanctions, adopted in a school's behaviour management policy, rather than any physical act.

An extension of operant conditioning which we must also consider briefly is the concept of programmed learning. Despite the obvious contemporary link with ICT in the name, this idea was not originally linked to computer use, but was a more general view on how learning could be developed. An example of this approach could be where children have been given some information which is then tested. Next,

> *a correct response was rewarded in some way (typically with praise); an incorrect response would lead to their being given either a repeat of the original information, or an alternative (simpler) presentation. Programmed learning was often implemented in expensive 'teaching machines' which presented the materials in the appropriate sequence. (Long, 2007, p15)*

One of the implications of the rapid advances in ICT technology discussed above, is that such 'machines' (in the forms of computers or many other devices) are now readily available in classroom, and indeed many homes, at an affordable cost. In this context, we need to consider carefully when, or if, it is appropriate to use them as 'teaching machines' in the process of Computer Assisted Learning (CAL).

Distinction between classical and operant conditioning

Although there are many more subtle distinctions, the key difference between classical and operant conditioning for our purposes is the nature of the response. In classical conditioning the response is involuntary and not under conscious control (such as heart rate), whereas in operant conditioning the response is voluntary and under conscious control (such as the behaviour of a child to get praise from a teacher).

Behaviourism, learners and ICT

Transmission

In a behaviourist view of learning, the 'minds of learners are seen as spaces to be filled, their objective is to accumulate knowledge of this world and the teacher's task to interpret and transmit this to the learners.' (Cook, 2010, p39) The idea of 'transmission' of information is central to understanding this model of learning and to how it links to ICT. In earlier chapters we have already seen that ICT is good at transmitting information (such as through a video) and we have also noted that ICT can do this quickly, using a range of different modes and media. However, just because ICT can do this, it does not necessarily make it a suitable use in learning and teaching. While there are times when teachers need to 'transmit' information (such as the details of a task), in most contemporary primary classrooms this would be limited. One of the main reasons for this is the belief of many teachers that the classroom should be a more democratic place (see 'Expeiential Learning' below).

WHAT DO YOU THINK?

When, if at all, is it appropriate to 'transmit' information or ideas? In deciding this you may want to consider if it varies by age of pupils, subject / area of learning, location (e.g. in classroom or outside) or school factors (such as approaching tests).

Stimulus and response

The other central idea of behaviourism we need to consider in relation to ICT is that of stimulus and response, which we will consider alongside programmed learning. As above, this is also an area where the features of ICT (See Chapter 1) can make it very effective, but can also impose limitations. Unlike humans, a computer's ability to respond time and again is only limited by technical reliability, rather than boredom or other more human factors. This can, however, also be a fundamental limitation. Anyone involved in interactions with a learner in a primary classroom would not actually want to keep responding in the same way. They would realise that they need to modify their response to take account of a range of factors, such as the level of learner engagement or their ability to understand what was being asked of them. Indeed, the sheer variety of responses offered by an experienced classroom practitioner, and the subtle nuances of response they can adapt to, cannot be matched (at least at the moment!) by a computer, or other ICT resource, however well programmed. Hopefully, the result is that the learner remains interested, rather than potentially becoming bored or disenchanted by the programmed responses of a computer. Indeed, Papert (1993, p19) provides an important warning of the dangers of 'the computer programming the child' in a situation where 'the computer is used to put children through their paces, to provide exercises of an appropriate level of difficulty, to provide feedback and to dispense information'. Advances in technology mean this warning now applies to many other ICT devices as well as computers, and as teachers we must be mindful that we are selecting ICT resources which allow children some control over their own learning.

Reward and sanction

We have seen above that rewards and sanctions are an essential feature of operant conditioning in human behaviour. The ability to offer these is, however, not restricted to humans. One of the ways that ICT resources help to avoid boredom (and potentially increase motivation) is through the use of rewards, and even sanctions. The rewards can range from reaching a new level, taking ownership of a new monster or printed certificates, whilst sanctions can range from repeating a level through to more prosaic sound effects.

This should not be taken to mean that there is no place for stimulus and response with rewards and sanctions. What is suggested is that this use of ICT must be matched closely to the likely effectiveness. It may be that in learning, or assessing, basic number bonds or times tables, a limited use of this approach may be suitable; although it should not be offered as a replacement for more effective or creative approaches and its effectiveness should be closely monitored. One reason for monitoring closely, which is a direct outcome of the features of ICT (especially through experience of using computer and console games – see Chapter 1), is the fact that a learner can achieve an answer, or solution to a problem, through trial and error rather than through logic or reasoning. It is suggested that the likelihood of trial and error being used increases the longer a learner is left unsupervised or not monitored.

Constructivism

We have seen above that in behaviourist theories the learner is acted upon by others to achieve learning. The central idea of constructivist views of learning is that, although still focusing on the individual (as opposed to more social models of learning later), the learner takes a central role in constructing their own knowledge and understanding. The distinction is neatly summed up by Jones and Mercer (1993, p15), who state that:

> *whereas in operant conditioning the emphasis is on the learner 'being shaped' by the instructor, (or computer) through selective reinforcement, here [constructivism] the learner*

is seen as an active participant, who, in the course of learning is structuring his or her experience or knowledge.

As with behaviourism above, we need to consider briefly two main areas of constructivism – cognitive constructivism and social constructivism – in general terms before moving to consider they apply to ICT.

Cognitive constructivism

Much of the work in this area is based on the ideas of Piaget and the early work of Bruner in the first half of the twentieth century. Cognitive constructivists consider how the individual learner develops knowledge, as opposed to social constructivism which is based on examining social relations in learning – see more below. For our purpose we will concentrate on the views of Piaget and his stages of cognitive development – 'ages and stages'. We do not need to cover each stage in detail as this has been covered by many writers elsewhere, but we do need to recognise the key principles of this stage theory:

- each stage has specific characteristics and is associated with a specific age range from birth to age 15;
- a child cannot 'jump' stages but must pass through all of them;
- as children grow older their ability to conceptualise develops.

In this theory, learning is closely linked to the stage of development and is a cumulative process. Given that one stage is built upon the preceding one, and 'if, therefore, cognitive frameworks depend on what had preceded,it is important to regulate the difficultly level and order of presentation of material'. (Child, 2007, p103) The judgement about difficulty may be a professional one, but there is a role for ICT in helping to order the presentation of material.

In terms of ICT, it is not difficult to see the influence of the stages of development in the labeling of, for instance, software as age specific.

WHAT DO YOU THINK?

Should we, as teachers accept such labels, or make our own judgment based on ability or experience? Or, indeed, should we allow children to make their own judgments?

In terms of differentiation, it is also important to note that children with additional learning needs may not fit such categories neatly. Overall, the theoretical Piagetian link between age and development may be less important in making decisions about the use of ICT resources, such as a piece of software, than professional judgment based on the reality of the child in your class regardless of their age – particularly given the increasing exposure of very young children to sophisticated ICT in the home prior to formal schooling examined in Chapter 4.

To explore further how Piaget's theory can be linked to ICT, it is necessary to also examine his views on how knowledge is structured in schemata. Each schema allows a child to hold a cognitive representation of something. These concepts would vary from child to child, but would be based on perceived important properties of the idea represented. For instance, a bird schema may be that birds can fly, have two wings and two legs. As the child adds new knowledge to the bird schema, for instance by seeing high definition pictures of the shape of different bird wings though the use of ICT, a process of assimilation takes place. Such a change will not change the fundamental property that birds have two wings. There will, however, also be occasions where a child discovers something, such as a bird that does not fly, which does not fit into the properties of the existing schema and means it must be changed. These changes are known as accommodation and can again be influenced by experience gained through ICT by, for instance, seeing movies of penguins on the IWB.

Although hugely influential, Piaget's theories have also been criticised due, amongst other reasons, to the close relationship of achievement with biological age, rather than the influence of the wider world in which the child lives and how this may impact at any age. This may be particularly true of experience of ICT, where children's ICT skills may be well in advance of other skills and greater than we may expect of someone of their age. The impact of the wider world, and those that inhabit it, led to the development of social constructivist theories.

Social constructivism: Socio-cultural theory

When considering both behaviourist and cognitive theories above, it should be noted that both theories focus on the leaner as an individual, isolated from their social context – even if working with others. In reality, as Jones and Mercer (1993, p20) rightly assert, learning 'may seem a solitary endeavour, but in practice nearly all learning (of computer skills or anything else) is in some sense a social experience: some person – colleague, tutor, manual author – is involved as well as the learner'. They continue to suggest that we cannot just consider theories of learning, but need to examine theoretical frameworks which take account of 'teaching-and-learning'. In this model of teaching-and-learning, great emphasis is placed on the ability of all involved to communicate with each other. In this book, this includes the ability to do this using a variety of communication tools to work with others who may not be physically present, using both synchronous (in real time) and/or or asynchronous (at different times) technologies. The advantages of real time communication (such as immediate response) are perhaps more apparent, but Conole and Dyke (2004) also point out the advantages of asynchronous technologies, such as blogs, which are being used in primary schools today. They suggest that such technologies have 'the potential for encouraging reflection and critique, with users engaging in discussions over a longer time frame than is possible in face-to-face discussions. In addition, users are able to access and build on archived material available from earlier discussion'. (Conole and Dyke, 2004, p118)

We should note that in these situations those involved in the learning are not communicating with, or expecting a response from, the computer (or other ICT tool), but with and from another learner – the ICT is not the object of the interaction, but a tool to interact though (see p. 16). The ICT resource, although capable of giving pre-programmed responses or lots of information, is a medium which 'reorganises interactions among people, creating new environments in which children can be educated and grow by gaining access to the world around them'. (Jones and Mercer, 1993, p23) With recent advances in using ICT, such as voice recognition, touch sensitive screens and gesture recognition, such opportunities are available to children of all ages and abilities.

The ideas of socio-cultural theory, in particular the work of Vygotsky, provide a suitable framework to analyse and discuss how ICT can contribute to a socio-constructivist view of teaching and learning.

Vysgotsky

Although relatively little known in the west until after his death in 1934, Vygotsky's influence has grown in recent years. (McIntyre, 2000) He was familiar with behaviourist theories and with the work of Piaget but

> *took issue with the Piagetian view that from the time of their birth children learn independently by exploring the environment, and with the behaviourist view that adults are entirely responsible for shaping children's learning by the judicious use of rewards and punishments. (Williams and Burden, 1997, p39, cited by Pachler, 1999)*

One of the key differences with the ideas of Piaget is that Vygotsky draws attention to the *potential achievement* of a child, particularly when collaborating with others, rather than his or her *independent achievement*. Unlike Piaget's conception that cognitive development precedes learning, Vygotsky (1978, p90) suggests that 'the development process lags behind the learning process; this sequence then results in zones of proximal development' (ZPD). Although these zones may differ in size between individuals (an important part of this theory for teachers to remember), the key idea is that the learner has the potential to make progress if working with 'adult guidance or in collaboration with more capable peers'. (Vygotsky, 1978, p86) As such, Jarvis et al., (2008, p37) propose that 'we cannot draw inferences from what individuals do independently. We need to try and see their potential rather than their achievements'. When considering the use of ICT in the primary school, or indeed at any stage of learning, we need to consider how it can facilitate this type of collaboration, and hence help fulfil potential. It is suggested, however, that this change in role does not diminish the role of the teacher in any way; in fact, it may even call for greater skill or the development of new skills. The ability to judge the size of the ZPD for each child, as well as making judgements about who may be classified as a more capable peer, or when to use adults instead, call for both skill and professional judgement on the part of the teacher, as well as an understanding of how ICT can be used effectively in this context.

Constructivism, learners and ICT

It was noted earlier that it is sometimes hard to see evidence of what learners know and how they learned it. Although children can be explicitly asked to explain an answer or a viewpoint, there may be many barriers (dependent on age and ability) that may prevent them giving an explanation which reflects their true understanding. This is particularly true when an answer has been arrived at in collaboration with others. One of the features of using ICT in the primary school in a constructivist approach, however, is that it can help make visible things that children know – for instance through the use of the interactive whiteboard room in a class discussion or concept mapping exercise – which would not be apparent otherwise. Recent studies (for example, Warwick and Kershner, 2008; Mercer, Hennessy and Warwick, 2010) have shown that using the IWB in particular (and other ICT resources) can be a very valuable way of supporting pupils' learning through, for instance, increased participation, motivation and sharing of ideas.

CASE STUDY

A KS2 class were studying the Second World War. A local landmark has been bombed and the class had a copy of a letter from a child who had lived near enough to see what happened. The teacher used the IWB flip chart software to display a section of a letter on the IWB showing what the child had written describing the events and the aftermath – the pupils would later get paper copies of the whole letter. In the text of the letter, the teacher had inserted hyperlinks to images of the landmark before and after the bombing and other links to images of local landmarks that were mentioned in the letter. The teacher had also inserted a link to a map of the area on another page of the flipchart. The teacher had got another child in the school to read the extract and had digitally recorded it so that when the text was clicked on the IWB the extract was read by a child of the same age as the writer. This was used at the beginning of the lesson to introduce the topic. The pupils then clicked on the links to view the images. At the same time the teacher used another blank page of the 'flip chart' for the pupils to write key words and phrases for later written work. The pupils then used the IWB pens to annotate the map showing where the bombs had been dropped based on the evidence from the letter. They discussed how this would have affected the area and the people that lived there throughout this work with the IWB. This dialogue and participation was the main focus of the lesson, but the ICT tools motivated and enhanced the lesson. Most of the same things could be done using posters, printed pictures and bits of paper, but the ICT automated this process allowing the work to be quicker, with better-quality images that could be seen by the whole class, with participation by all and done in one place with the IWB as a 'digital hub'– see more in Chapter 6 – for accessing a variety of modes and media.

The use of ICT in collaborative work can also allow opportunities to facilitate tasks addressing the ZPD identified by Vygotsky, although this can also be done with more traditional resources. The guiding principle is that, as stated before, ICT should be used when it can do things better and/or quicker than other resources.

Experience-based learning – John Dewey

The idea that learners can take an active role in supporting each other, for instance in ZPD activities above, is also a feature of democratic pedagogy, originating from the ideas of the American John Dewey in the late nineteenth and early twentieth centuries. Alexander (2008, p80) sums up democratic pedagogy as rejecting

> *the traditional domination – subordination relationship between teacher and taught, makes knowledge reflexive rather than disciplinary, the child an active agent in his or her own learning, and the classroom a workshop or laboratory. In all these aspects the classroom seeks to enact the ideals of the wider democratic society. Negotiation thus stands in conscious antithesis to both transmission and induction.*

Dewey's influence, particularly in America, was significant as part of what became known as the Progressive movement. In *The School and Society*, published in 1899, Dewey proposed a 'new 'education' based on a 'conception of experience-based practical learning [which would] form habits of inquiry and co-operation securing democratic life'. (Waks in Dewey, 2001, p387) The concept of negotiation is central to understanding this theory, and learners take an active role in their own learning with the ability to influence decisions. This idea was to influence constructivist and other theories which followed. In 1921, Schneider (1921, p136 cited in Brehoney, 1997, p429) introduced Dewey's idea to British readers as follows:

> *The emphasis on natural development is supposed to come directly from Rousseau. The idea of 'learning by doing' is attributed largely to Pestalozzi. The educational use of play is attributed largely to Froebel and the idea of freedom to Montessori.*

By building on these ideas, Dewey suggested that children should learn in a democratic classroom through

> *purposive and conscious activity; not Froebel's 'drawing out' nor Herbart's 'putting in' but rather the giving of direction to pupils' activities. These activities were held to arise from impulses or instincts which could be classified into four groups which were available for guidance in the school. These Dewey labelled, the social instinct, the instinct of making, the instinct of investigation and the expressive impulse.*
> *(Brehony, 1997, p435)*

What should be apparent by now is that the features of ICT can cater for all of these groups and, indeed, they provide an appropriate framework for classifying ICT activities.

Activity

Using the following headings, identify ICT activities in different areas of learning or subjects:

The social instinct	**The instinct for making**	**The instinct for investigation**	**The expressive impulse**

Experiential learning

Dewey's idea contributed to the centrality of learner's experience in their own learning, developing the notion of child-centred learning. The concept of experiential learning, however, is on one level very simple (in that we will apprehend the world around us as we learn, whether planned or unplanned), but also complex (each person's experience is different and subjective). In examining the ideas of Dewey we have taken a slightly narrow view of experiential learning, but this is deliberate as we are accepting Jarvis et al.'s (2003) suggestion that *all* learning is experiential in some way. They suggest rightly that the term 'experiential learning' has become a 'new orthodoxy' and, as such, is largely redundant except when educators deliberately plan learning 'in which the learner's have primary experience of the external world'. (Jarvis et al., 2003, p67) In this view, ICT may appear to have little to offer, except when the ICT forms part of the real world – although it does reinforce the importance of presenting ICT in 'real' contexts. If we only accept primary experience, however, we are losing important experiences which can be gained through mediated experience. It is in this context that ICT can play an important part in experiential learning.

Multiple intelligences – Gardner

The four instinct groups identified above when considering the ideas of Dewey, also provide an early precursor to the idea that children may have instincts, or intelligences, in more than one area. Much later, in 1983, Howard Gardner published 'Frames of Mind' which, he later stressed, he wrote as a 'psychologist and thought that he was addressing principally his colleagues in psychology. He devoted little of the book to educational implications and never expected that his ideas would be picked up by educators, first in the United States and then, eventually, in many countries across the globe'. (Gardner, 2008, p1) Despite this, his 'theory of multiple intelligences' (MI theory) (rather than a single, unitary intelligence) has become very influential in educational settings. As much has been written on this elsewhere, for our purposes it is only necessary to list his original intelligences[1]:

1. Linguistic intelligence
2. Logical-mathematical intelligence
3. Musical intelligence
4. Bodily-kinesthetic intelligence
5. Spatial intelligence Interpersonal intelligence
6. Intrapersonal intelligence
7. Interpersonal intelligence

[1]Gardner added an 'eighth (naturalist) intelligence and continues to speculate about a possible ninth (existential) intelligence'. (Gardner, 2008)

It is important to note immediately, however, that due to the popularity of Gardner's ideas in educational circles, there have been many interpretations of his original ideas. As he did not consider himself an educator, Gardner (2008) asserts he 'did not lay out – and indeed never has laid out- a program for the education of multiple intelligences'. However, to mark the 25th anniversary of his ideas, and to counter some 'radical abuse' of his ideas, he did write about 'the various myths and misunderstanding of MI theory – for example, confusing an intelligence with a learning style, or asserting that all children are strong in at least one intelligence'. Given the common use of VAK (Visual–Audio–Kinesthetic) ideas in primary school, often based on the assumption that MI can help identify learning styles, some may be surprised by the first myth, but it should encourage us to read first-hand materials wherever possible – see more in Chapter 6.

For the purposes of this chapter it is also important to note that Gardner (2008) continues to suggest that he 'now believes that any serious application of MI ideas should entail at least two components:

1. An attempt to individuate education as much as possible. The advent of personal computers should make this goal much easier to attain.
2. A commitment to convey important ideas and concepts in a number of different formats. This activation of multiple intelligences holds promise of reaching many more students and also demonstrating what it means to understand a topic thoroughly and deeply'.

Whilst the role of ICT in the first component is explicit (and should not be restricted to computers), we should also recognise from previous chapters that the ability to present ideas and concepts using a variety of modes and media is also strength of ICT. Perhaps the most important idea to take forward to the next chapters is that Gardner's ideas relate to the *potential* existence of more than one intelligence, and the role of ICT should be to *activate* these intelligences, rather than be employed trying to satisfy or facilitate supposed learning styles. Indeed, Gardner himself (2008) suggests that one of the ways in which MI theory could expand is in the 'devising of computer software and virtual realities that present or teach the same topics via the activation of several intelligences'.

Even if you do not believe in the existence of Multiple Intelligences (MIs), using them as a framework to ensure you exploit all the facilities of ICT may be a useful activity. In figure 3.1, p42 a start has been made on such an exercise.

ACTIVITY

In groups, or on your own, add more ICT activities, resources or programs to the outer boxes in the diagram p42.

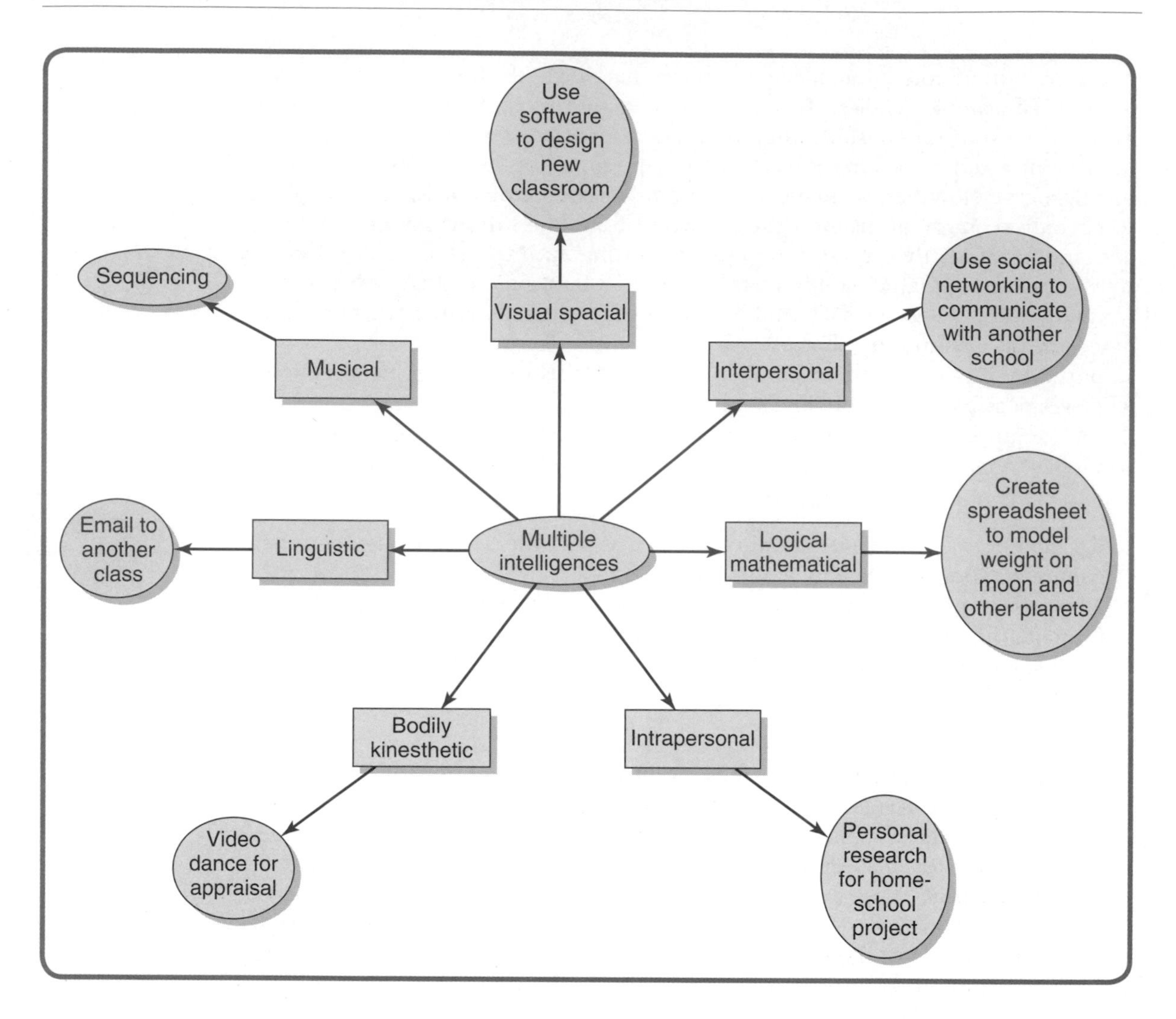

Figure 3.1 Multiple intelligences and ICT

Goals of instruction – theory into practice

Given the multitude and complexity of the theories explored above, it is should be obvious that no one theory will cater for every situation. As in all aspects of teaching, in reality you will start with the learning you want to achieve and then decide the best way of attaining it. Although aimed at those designing educational software, Dabbagh (undated) provides a useful summary of how the theories examined above can be linked to the outcomes of lessons using ICT – see website for more information. This table uses three competing schools of thought summarised by Dede (2008, p45) as

1. Objectivism posits that reality is external and is objective, and knowledge is gained through experiences. Behaviorists believe that, since learning is based on experience, instructions centres are manipulating environmental factors to create instructional events inculcating content and procedures in ways that alters students' behaviours.
2. Pragmatism posits that reality is mediated through cognitively developed representations, and knowledge is negotiated through experience and thinking. Cognitivists believe that, since learning involves both experience and thinking, instruction centres on helping learners develop interrelated, symbolic mental constructs that form the basis of knowledge and skills.
3. Interpretivism posits that reality is internal, and knowledge is constructed. Constructivists believe that, since learning involves constructing one's own knowledge, instruction centres on helping learners to actively invent individual meaning from experience.

Each of these schools of thought should not be regarded as a single unified theory, but a collection of theories loosely related by a common set of fundamental assumptions. The major theorists for each school of thought who have been examined above are listed in table 3.2 – see Dabbagh (undated) for more theorists and full version of the table.

Although there may be times when the teacher uses all of these schools of thought, it is suggested that most ICT use (especially in an interactive or dialogic classroom) will be based on constructivist views listed in the final column.

Table 3.2 Dabbagh's Instructional Design Knowledge Base (IDKB)

Principal Theorists		
Objectivism/Behaviorism	**Cognitivism/Pragmatism**	**Constructivism/Interpretivism**
Pavlov Skinner	Gardner	Bruner Dewey Papert Piaget Vygotsky

(continued)

Goals of Instruction

Objectivism / Behaviorism	Cognitivism/Pragmatism	Constructivism/Interpretivism
• Communicate or transfer behaviors representing knowledge and skills to the learner (does not consider mental processing) • Instruction is to elicit the desired response from the learner who is presented with a target stimulus • Learner must know how to execute the proper response as well as the conditions under which the response is made • Learner acquires skills of discrimination (recalling facts), generalisation (defining and illustrating concepts), association (applying explanations), and chaining (automatically performing a specified procedure).	• Communicate or transfer knowledge in the most efficient, effective manner (mind-independent, can be mapped onto learners) • Focus of instruction is to create learning or change by encouraging the learner to use appropriate learning strategies • Learning results when information is stored in memory in an organised, meaningful way. • Teachers/designers are responsible for assisting learners in organising information in an optimal way so that it can be readily assimilated	• Build personal interpretations of the world based on individual experiences and interactions (constantly open to change, cannot achieve a predetermined, 'correct' meaning, knowledge emerges in relevant contexts) • Learning is an active process of constructing rather than acquiring knowledge • Instruction is a process of supporting knowledge construction rather than communicating knowledge • Do not structure learning for the task, but engage learner in the actual use of the tools in real world situations • Learning activities should be authentic and should center around the "problematic" or 'puzzlement' as perceived by the learner • The focus is on the process not the product • Role of teacher is a mentor not a 'teller' • Encourage reflective thinking, higher-order learning skills • Encourage testing viability of ideas and seeking alternative views

Source: adapted from Dabbagh (undated) **http://tinyurl.com/34vkvmh**[2]

[2]All references from this page onwards use **www.tinyurl.com** to shorten very long urls to more manageable length. This can be useful in presentations.

SUMMARY

In this chapter we have focussed on learners and how they learn. This has been set in the context of how ICT can contribute to the needs of both an individual and the society in which they live; as well the need in some to gain formal knowledge for its own sake. In achieving these diverse aims we have also examined a range of learning theories and related them to a range of ICTs. From this, it has become apparent that ICT can contribute to personalised, socially situated and experiential learning by providing a range of tools and enhancing motivation. Overall, it is suggested that no single theory of learning can be applied to all learners, but that ICT can be applied to a greater or lesser extent in all. It is suggested that the effectiveness of its use can be increased if teachers consider carefully the theoretical context in which it is being used.

References

Alexander, R. (2008), *Essays on Pedagogy*, Abingdon: Routledge.

Brehony, K.J. (1997) 'An "undeniable" and "Disastrous" Influence? Dewey and English education (1895–1939)', *Oxford Review of Education*, 23(4), pp427–45.

Child, D. (2007), *Psycholgy and the Teacher*, 8th edition, London: Continuum.

Coffield, F., Moseley, D., Hall, E. and, Ecclestone, K. (2004), *Should We Be using Learning Styles? What Research has to Say to Practice*, Learning and Skills Research Centre, Trowbridge: Cromwell. Press.

Conole, G. and Dyke, M. (2004), 'What are the affordances of information and communication technologies?', *ALT J, Research in Learning Technology*, Vol.12, No. 2, pp113–24.

Cook, D. (2010), 'Views of learning, assessment and the potential place of information technology', in McDougall, A. (ed) *Researching IT in Education: Theory, Practice and Future* Directions, London: Routledge, pp39–45.

Dabbagh (undated) **http://tinyurl.com/34vkvmh** (accessed on 16.01.12)

Dede, C. (2008) 'Theoretical frameworks influencing the use of Information Technolgy in teaching and learning', in Voogt, J. and Knezek, G. (2008), *International Handbook of Information Technology in Primary and Secondary Education*, Volume 20, New York: Springer, pp43–62.

Dewey, John (2001), 'The educational situation: as concerns the elementary school', *Journal of Curriculum Studies*, 33(4), pp387–403.

Gardner, H. (1983), *Frames of Mind: The Theory of Multiple Intelligences*, New York: Basic Books.

Gardner, H. (2003), 'Multiple intelligences after twenty years', **http://www.howardgardner.com/Papers/papers.html** (accessed 10.10.11).

Gardner, H. (2008), 'The 25th anniversary of the publication of Howard Gardner's *Frames of Mind: The Theory of Multiple Intelligences*, **http://www.howardgardner.com/Papers/papers.html** (Accessed 10.10.11)

Howard-Jones, P. (2007), *Neuroscience and Education: Issues and Opportunities, A Commentary by the Teaching and Learning Research Programme*, London: TLRP.

Howard-Jones, P. (2009), *Neuroscience, Learning and Technology (14–19)*, for Deep Learning Project, London: BECTA.

Jarvis, P., Holford, J. and Griffin, C. (2003), *The Theory and Practice of Learning*, 2nd edition, London: Routledge Falmer.

Jones, A. and Mercer, N. (1993), 'Theories of learning and information technology', in Scrimshaw, P. (ed.) (1993).

Kelly, A.V. (2009), *The Curriculum* (6th edition), London: Sage.

Long, M. (2007), *The Psychology of Education*, London: RoutledgeFalmer.

McIntyre, D. (2000), 'The nature of classroom teaching expertise,' in Whitebread, David. (ed.) (2000), *The Psychology of Teaching and Learning in the Primary School*, London: Routledge Falmer. pp1–14.

Meadows, S. (2004), 'Models of cognition in childhood: metaphors, achievements and problems', in *The Routledge Falmer Reader in Psychology of Education.* London: Routledge.

Mercer, N., Hennessy, S. and Warwick, P. (2010), 'Using interactive whiteboards to orchestrateclassroom dialogue', Technology, *Pedagogy and Education*, 19(2), 195–209.

Organisation for Economic Co-operation and Development (2001), *Understanding the Digital Divide.* Retrieved from **http://www.oecd.org/**

Pachler, N. (1999), 'Theories of Learning and ICT', in Leask, M. and Pachler, N. *Learning to Teach Using ICT in the Secondary School*, London: Routledge.

Pavlov, I. (1927), *Conditioned Reflexes*, Oxford: Milford.

Prensky, M. (2001), 'Digital natives, digital immigrants', *On the Horizon*, *9*(5), pp1–6.

Scrimshaw, P. (ed.) (1993), *Language, Classrooms and Computers*, London: Routledge.

Sharp, J.G., Byrne, J. and Bowker, R. (2008), 'The trouble with VAK', *Educational Futures*, Vol.1(1), August 2008, 89–97.

Skinner, B. (1938), *The Behavior of Organisms*, New York: Appleton Century Crofts.

Vygotsky, L. (1978), *Mind in Society*, Cambridge, MA: Harvard University Press.

Warwick, P. and Kershner, R. (2008) 'Primary teachers' understanding of the interactive whiteboard as a tool for children's collaborative learning and knowledge-building', *Learning, Media and Technology*, 33(4), pp269–87.

Woollard, J. (2010), *Psychology for the Classroom: Behaviourism*, London: Routledge.

Woolfolk, A., Hughes, M. and Walkup, V. (2008), *Psychology in Education*, Harlow: Pearson.

Yeomans, J. and Arnold, C. (2006), *Teaching, Learning and Psychology*, London: David Fulton.

CHAPTER 4

ICT and the Teacher: Pupils, Planning and Inclusion

In this chapter we will consider how teachers use ICT based on the needs of *all* pupils who have grown up in a world surrounded by technology and may be considered 'digital natives'. We will examine the potential impact of this under the headings of planning and preparation in an inclusive classroom. The chapter ends with an examination of e-safety.

Start with the child

Given the huge growth in both the number and variety of ICT devices available, coupled with their relatively low price, it is inevitable that children arrive in school with some experience of ICT. In Chapter 5 we will examine the implications for this for early years classes, but there are also issues that need to be considered throughout the primary school. One of the most important of these is the potential for children in the class to have greater personal experience of, and capability in, the use of ICT than their teachers due to their exposure to ICT from birth.

Any figures provided in this chapter regarding how many children have access to ICT resources will become outdated very quickly. Therefore, to represent a baseline, and with the assumption that numbers will only increase, we will consider the findings of Selwyn, Potter and Cranmer (2009) who conducted research with 612 pupils in five primary schools in the London and West Midlands regions of England the 2007–08 academic year. The results are important as the schools were selected to force variation in terms of pupils' ethnicity, geo-demographic and socio-economic factors and included two inner city schools and two suburban schools in London and one school in a medium/small town located in the West Midlands. Overall, Selwyn, Potter and Cranmer (2009, p922) report that

> *89% (n = 543) of respondents reported having access to a computer that was available to them to use if they required. Eighty-six per cent (n = 523) of respondents reported having access to a games console (e.g., Wii, Xbox, PS3), 61% (n = 376) access to their own television in their bedroom and 51% (n = 314) a mobile phone that they could use if required. … these levels of access increased by the age of the respondent, with older children more likely to report access to all four of these ICTs.*

This type of wide access to ICT supports the notion of children as 'digital natives'. This term was first used by Prensky (2001) as a result of his views that rapid advances in ICT represented a 'singularity'; that is 'an event which changes things so fundamentally that there is absolutely no going back. This so-called "singularity" is the arrival and rapid dissemination of digital technology in the last decades of the 20th century." (Prensky, 2001, p1) Prensky was writing about the generation of children who were in education (from nursery to university) at the time of writing, who had grown up with ICT around them from birth and as a result were 'all "native speakers" of the digital language of computers, video games and the Internet'. (Prensky, 2001, p1) He continued to suggest that this generation had a fundamentally different approach to thinking and processing information, compared to the rest of the population who he labelled 'digital immigrants'. He suggested that if digital immigrants wish to teach digital natives effectively, they would have to 'stop their grousing' (p6) and change. If you agree with this view, the situation can only have developed further in the years since.

It has to be said, however, that not everybody agrees with the need for change in this context. Bennett et al., (2008, p776) go so far as to suggest that whilst 'calls for major change in education are being widely propounded, they have been subjected to little critical scrutiny, are undertheorised, and lack a sound empirical basis'. They continue to suggest that, whilst more 'dispassionate research' is needed, 'the picture beginning to emerge from research on young people's relationships with technology is much more complex than the digital native characterisation suggests. While technology is embedded in their lives, young people's use and skills are not uniform'. (Bennett et al, 2008, p783)

ACTIVITY

Do you consider the children that you teach to be 'digital natives'? *Consider this question on your own, or discuss with others. You may wish to reflect on what factors (such as age or social background) affect your decision and whether the ICT resources available to pupils in school either exacerbate or improve this situation. You may also wish to consider whether* **you** *are a digital native and the impact of this on the way you see technology being used in teaching.*

Computer use in the home

Although an increasing number of households have access to computers, they also have access to a wide variety of other ICT devices both static and mobile – although social inequalities remain (Organisation for Economic Co-operation and Development [OECD], 2001; Ofcom, 2010). When allied to increased access to high speed broadband internet connections, children have access to a range of networks both within the home and beyond. The ways in which these ICT resources are used, however, presents a tension between parental aspirations, for instance to support homework (Cranmer, 2006), and children's actual use, largely game-based. This relative freedom in ICT at home can lead primary children to make negative comparisons with more constrained ICT in educational settings. In a recent study of Key Stage 2 (KS2) children, Selwyn et al., (2009, p924) found that the children's views 'reflect clearly the restrictions of the schools and the (relative) freedoms of the home, as well as the oppositional relationship between the "work" of learning in school and the "play" of using digital media at home'. Even within the 'restrictions' of school ICT use, Kerawalla and Crook (2006, p751) found that school technology

> *is well placed to extend children's opportunities for learning. However, computers are versatile tools: they support a wider range of activities than those that are prominent in classrooms. Whatever parents who purchase computers may hope to encourage at home, research suggests that, for most children, game playing becomes the predominant form of domestic use.*

As we have already discussed computers games and their impact (see Chapter 1), the main point to consider here is that, as we have already seen, children will not necessarily use ICT in the way you intend them to. This is not necessary a subversive activity, but merely a reflection but how they perceive ICT and use it in out of school settings.

It may also be a reflection of children's competence in ICT use. Nearly a decade ago, Pearson and Somekh (2003, p21) found that primary school pupils were in an ideal position to acquire a range of skills in the use of ICT provided they have access to ICT tools, and would be capable of using these tools to support their own autonomous learning. Given the speed of developments and the sophistication of contemporary ICT resources, it seems unlikely that children are any less prepared to use such tools today.

Whichever view you take on the issues above, it is impossible to dispute that rapid, and ever more sophisticated, developments in ICT resources will have an impact of some kind on learning and teaching, especially for teachers who have to adapt to an ever increasing range of technology. To provide the structure for this chapter we will consider the potential impact, and possible solutions, of these changes under the headings of planning and preparation.

Planning

There are many styles and formats of planning (see, for example, Grigg, 2010) but for our purposes we need to consider how ICT can be used effectively in the planning process and what factors we need to consider to use ICT effectively. It is important, however, that we consider the use of ICT in the context of broader issues which need to be considered in the planning process. We have already considered theories of learning, but we also need to examine issues surrounding learning styles and ICT.

Learning styles

Although not a theory of learning, when planning we need to reflect on the impact of learning styles in education and the role of ICT within them. A learning style may be defined as 'as a set of learner characteristics that influences their response to different teaching approaches'. (Howard-Jones, 2009, p29) The main problem when considering learning styles is not only the abundance of models, but also the competing academic and commercial benefits of successful use, which can lead to their promotion at the expense of proven merit. Coffield et al., (2004, p2) identify 71 different models and highlight that 'beneath the apparently unproblematic appeal of learning styles lies a host of conceptual and empirical problems' to which we will return below.

The most popular categorisation of learning styles occurs when learners may be allocated to one of three types of learning style (Visual, Auditory or Kinaesthetic – VAK). From previous chapters we know that ICT has the capability to provide high quality visual and auditory materials. We also know that we should not confuse learning styles with possible intelligences. However, in a summary of research on neuroscience and education for the Teaching and Learning Research Programme (TLRP), Howard-Jones (2007, p16) states that 'some believe that presenting material in a way that suits an individual's preferred learning style can improve their learning. ... However, there is a considerable scarcity of quality research to support the value of identifying learning styles'. Indeed, the whole concept of Visual, Auditory and Kinaesthetic (VAK) learning in particular has many critics. Sharp, Byrne and Bowker (2008, p91) go so far as to assert that 'to the best of our knowledge, independently verified quasi-experimental and longitudinal studies producing conclusive evidence pointing unequivocally to such a close relationship between VAK and children's academic performance at primary school do not exist'. This is supported by Goswami and Bryant (2007, p20) who conclude that 'Learning by the brain depends on the development of multi-sensory networks of neurons distributed across the entire brain. For example, a concept in science may depend on neurons being simultaneously active in visual, spatial, memory, deductive and kinaesthetic regions, in both brain hemispheres. Ideas such as left-brain/right-brain learning, or unisensory "learning styles" (visual, auditory *or* kinaesthetic) are *not* supported by the brain science of learning'.

In this context, it is important to realise that although ICT can indeed provide high quality visual or aural stimuli, the justification for their use should not just be that they match a single learning style, particularly using a VAK model. Nevertheless, as Howard-Jones (2007, p16) concludes

> *of course, this does not detract from the general value for all learners when teachers present learning materials using a full range of forms and different media. Such an approach can engage the learner and support their learning processes in many different ways, but the existing research does not support labelling children in terms of a particular learning style.*

The facility of ICT to provide such a full range of forms and media is one of its strengths and, as such, considering how it can exploit a range of learning styles, not just VAK, is an important starting point for ICT use in lesson planning.

Differentiation

Differentiation is a complex area, but is broadly conceived here as the ability to match the level or type of task to the known level, or potential level (see Vygotsky in Chapter 3), of each child. In broad terms we can also divide this into physical and cognitive differentiation, but in the primary school differentiation can take many forms – see Kerry and Kerry (1997) for a detailed discussion of pros and cons of many methods. Medwell (2007) suggests these include:

- Presentation
- Context
- Resources
- Grouping
- Task
- Support

In this list ICT could be regarded as a resource, but the use of ICT can also contribute to others – for example, how content is presented or provides a context for the work. In addition, ICT use can also facilitate group work (e.g. laptop for music composition, digital voice recorder for interviewing or IWB for planning a design task). The choice to use ICT, or not, can in itself be an act of differentiation, either to support less able learners or to stretch more the able, but this is only effective in a classroom where pupils are confident in using ICT independently. This type of pupil-centred learning environment with ICT is advocated by Smeets and Mooij (2001, p416), who suggest that

> *Teachers need to create learning environments that are adapted to the needs, abilities, and interests of individual pupils, thus stimulating pupils to be active, to co-operate and to take more responsibility for the learning processes. ICT may not be expected to contribute to creating innovative, pupil-centred learning environments unless the teachers involved pay attention to the potential of ICT to facilitate curriculum differentiation. Teachers should adopt the role of a coach who actually hands over a substantial part of the responsibility for the learning processes to the pupils.*

If this approach is required, much work needs to be done at the planning stage, bearing in mind that just using ICT will not be enough. Instead, you need to remember the features of ICT previously discussed and decide to use only those features that make ICT a better choice than any other resource. In addition, having made the decision to use it, you need to make decisions based on the individual needs and abilities of your class. Like the actual work they may be undertaking, the type of ICT selected, the actual features of it to be used and access (e.g. overlay keyboards to change letters from upper to lower case – see 'ICT as enabler' below, p54) to them also needs to be differentiated.

Preparation

Classroom design / ICT resources

When visiting schools, it is obvious that the design and layout of both schools and classrooms varies immensely, dictated by many factors including their age, adaptations and equipment present. The physical layout of a classroom will obviously have an impact (both positive and negative) on opportunities for interaction. Some classrooms provide discrete areas for discussion in groups, whilst others provide large open spaces with easy access for pupils (and teachers) to move around and interact or hold whole class discussions, whilst others still (such as an L-shaped classroom) make interactions (pupils–pupil, pupil–teacher and pupil–technology) much more challenging. This 'architecture shaped discourse' (Beauchamp, 2011) and subsequent interactions need careful consideration. Unfortunately, not many teachers are in a position where they can choose to design and build a new classroom, so they have to make decisions about the best use of the space they have available. This is especially true of how they facilitate the use of ICT in the classroom, or make decisions to use it elsewhere. In some instances, the position of network points or power sockets make it difficult to achieve significant change, but this only applies to fixed resources, such PCs or IWBs. The increasing use of mobile technologies and their ability to connect to remote devices (such as printers and network storage) wirelessly, or to store work remotely on as network, or even access programs remotely using Cloud computing,makes the flexible use of ICT much easier.

WHAT IS CLOUD COMPUTING?

Cloud computing (or technology) allows users to access applications, resources or applications through a web browser rather than from software installed on whatever device they are working on. In addition, work can be saved remotely to ensure access from anywhere with an Internet connection. Many people use this technology already without realising it, for instance on blog or social networking websites, accessing their email on a web browser, or even on shopping sites such as Amazon. In reality, the 'cloud' is a network of computers which host the relevant software, which means that much less space is needed on the hardware devices. This leaves space available for other features and enables manufacturers to produce devices with less memory and hence smaller machines. Some cloud services are managed and hence have cost implications; but this also means that support is provided when things go wrong – and it can be resolved remotely as that is where the fault will lie. There are many advantages to such an approach, but also some drawbacks, the most fundamental being if you lose your Internet connection, you lose your access to the software or other resources or any work saved there. This may be less of a concern in fixed computers with wired network connections, such as in many classrooms currently, but may be more of a concern with mobile access to the Internet. In addition, there may also be security concerns as with any Internet-based work.

This increased flexibility should also help pupils to take more control over their learning as advocated above, as it will increase their ability to make decisions about not only what technology they use, but also where they use it. To artificially restrict pupils to one location, based solely on the availability of a power supply, seems rather contrary. In addition, given the location of many classroom computers, the thoughts of Stephen Heppell are worth considering when he states that 'sitting facing the wall was formerly a punishment and just adding a bit of technology doesn't change the social isolation and exclusion much'. (**http://rubble.heppell.net/places/#physical**) Based on experience in many countries, Heppell (see previous link and **www.heppell.net**) has many suggestions for modifying learning spaces (and wider ICT issues) ranging from simply adding mirrors to the wall behind computers (so that both learners and teachers can make eye contact without turning around) through to significant changes in classroom design and furniture.

In reality, most teachers will probably be faced with making the most of specific fixed ICT resources, before considering mobile devices. Perhaps the most common fixed resource will be the IWB and the first step in preparation of lessons with IWBs is to check it can be seen from all positions where pupils will sit. It is surprising how often pupils are too polite to say they can't see! Even if you have sat in their seat to check the IWB can be seen (an easy first step), the fact you are taller means you can see when they can't. The same concerns apply to the position of text (or anything else they need to see, like pictures) on materials for are presenting. In presentation tools such as PowerPoint it is possible to change the slide template you use to ensure that text does not appear below the line of sight and this is well worth considering. In addition, Egerton et al., (undated) suggest that 'students should be able to face the board straight on without having to angle their heads, to avoid reduced levels of concentration and the risk of muscle strain (Miller et al., 2004; Sharp, 2006). They need clear access to the IWB – anything which limits students' access to it may affect their inclination to contribute (Higgins et al., 2007)'.

ICT and inclusion

Another important part of planning and preparing for lessons is to consider inclusion and how ICT can contribute, particularly with pupils with SENs. To understand how ICT can help, we need to examine both the idea of inclusion itself and how its current understanding was arrived at.

Inclusion as a concept is deeply rooted in liberal and progressive thinking. Thomas, Walker and Webb (2005, p18) suggest that the 1944 Education Act, as well as providing free education for all, 'constructed a highly segregative post-war education system with its ten categories of handicap for which special schools would cater'. This resulted in a minority of pupils being placed in 'special' schools with the majority in 'mainstream' schools – although the selection process at age 11 (the '11-plus') ensured that even these schools were not part of a 'comprehensive' education system. The next move was to try to 'integrate' pupils with special needs into the mainstream system. The term integration was first used in education in 1988 (Thomas and Vaughan, 2004) but, since then, reflecting wider concerns over rights, participation and social justice outside of education, there has been a move away from 'integration' towards 'inclusion' for *all*. To be clear about the distinction between integration and inclusion, and how this may affect use of ICT, we need to briefly consider them in more detail. Jones (2004, p12) states that integration can be regarded as a 'state', which involves 'putting someone in where they were originally excluded'; but does just doing this mean they will be truly integrated? Integration can also be regarded as a 'process' with 'planned and continuous interaction with other children within common educational systems and settings' (ibid.). But, in the context of this book, we need to be aware that this ignores other interactions, for example, with ICT. Inclusion, on the other hand, may be:

1. an attitude or principle: redefineing 'normality' as accepting and valuing diversity
2. an end product: a non-segregated system of education (Jones, 2004, p13)

Both of these ideas also work at a class level, where work can be planned for pupils to have continuous interactions (between both human and other resources) in a classroom environment, where all are regarded as equal and having a right to equal access. The distinction between integration and inclusion is summed up by Woolfson (2011, p175) as 'with inclusion the mainstream school reorganises its structures to accommodate children regardless of their needs. Integration on other hand leaves the school structure unchanged and the child's task is to assimilate into an unchanged school environment'.

ICT as enabler

In this context, ICT can be an aid to moving from integration to inclusion. Rahamin (2004) makes the important point that ICT has a long tradition of supporting pupils with SEN in the mainstream classroom, by allowing such pupils to achieve something that would be very difficult or even impossible to achieve in any other way. This assistive, or enabling, technology includes touch screens, large track balls instead of a mouse, placing computers on adjustable trolleys so they could be lowered for wheelchair users and 'talking' word processors. Such changes as also known as technical accommodations and could also include 'assistive devices to help a student to communicate or to produce work output (e.g. modified keyboard, a computer with a visual display and touch screen or with voice synthesiser, braillers for blind students, greatly enlarged text ona computer screen for a student with partial sight, radio-frequency hearing aids for students with impaired hearing)'. (Westwood, 2005, pp155–156)

ACTIVITY

Discuss the use of any such devices you have witnessed in the classroom. Why have they been effective, if they have, and what factors can positively or negatively impact on their use?

If you have not seen or used such devices, undertake some research into as many as possible and share and discuss your findings with others.

E-inclusion

The whole area of using ICT to help with learning difficulties is complex, but could perhaps be summed up as trying to encourage what Abbot (2007) calls e-inclusion, which aims to use digital technologies to minimise the problems that pupils with learning difficulties experience. This is based on the social model of inclusion, where learning difficulties are created by the social context,rather than a medical model which sees the difficulties as biologically determined. Such a model resonates with collaborative models of learning with ICT explored in this book and Abbot outlined three categories for using digital technologies for e-inclusion:

- using technology to train or rehearse
- using technology to assist learning
- using technology to enable learning.

We have considered the limitations of using technology to train or rehearse, but we have, and will continue to, explore how technology can assist and enable learning. Although it is necessary to read the full report to gain a complete understanding, Abbot (2007, p2) concludes that

> *it is possible to recognise the limitations of drill and practice software and the potential of socially collaborative use of digital technologies. Although computers have been used to some effect to assist learners to practise skills, it is only when they have been employed to enable learning that the full potential of e-inclusion has begun to be revealed.*

To ensure this happens as much as possible, it is essential to use a diverse range of teaching styles and resources. This may be easier with some ICT resources than others, but even apparently beneficial ICT resources can have disadvantages. A good example of this is the IWB, which can present a range of multi-modal resources (thus potentially allowing access for some pupils with SEN), but also requires a level of fine motor control to use, particularly if the IWB requires a pen, which then count against it being included in an interactive teaching style with some pupils with SEN unless adaptations are made. In a review of IWB use with children with autism and complex learning disabilities, Egerton et al., (undated) concluded that, although the IWB motivated such pupils,

> *students with ASD and severe and complex learning disabilities often do not have the expressive communicative skills or executive skills to demonstrate or present understanding by ways other than physical manipulation of the IWB or the physical resources they are working with. Additionally, these students' need to focus on one aspect of learning at a time can dictate a linear and prescriptive teaching style. However, by employing a cumulative 'layering' approach whereby learning experiences in different modes are consecutively built up and, where possible, eventually combined, teaching staff can enrich students' learning experience.*

In reality, as above, there will be barriers which make inclusion with, and of, ICT difficult and these may be categorised as situational, institutional and dispositional (Harrison, 1993). Teachers, unless they are senior managers, may find it difficult to directly influence institutional policy, but they can deal with the situational (the classroom, including ICT use) and the dispositional (professional characteristics and relations with pupils, including willingness to allow pupils to use ICT even if the teacher lacks confidence). If we assume that everyone reading this book has suitable dispositional characteristics, we can turn to consider situational factors.

In the classroom context, ICT can be used in a variety of ways and each needs to be considered when planning. We have considered many factors in earlier chapters, but specifically in relation to inclusion we will consider how ICT can:

- be used to tutor or to explore;
- be applied as a tool
- be used to communicate.

In addition, in SEN, ICT is also used for assessment and management purposes. (Means, 1994), to which we will return below.

ICT as tutor

ICT can offer individual(ised) instruction, but its effectiveness will depend on the match of this instruction to the needs of the learners. Indeed, 'in an extensive review of the literature on technology research in special education, Woodward and Rieth (1997) reported mixed results for the use of computer programs to generate feedback to pupils with SEN. They concluded that, on its own, Computer-assisted Instruction (CAI) was insufficient for teaching pupils with SEN. However, individualised learning programs retain their appeal, particularly as a supplementary support for learners with special educational needs'. (Florian and Hegarty, 2004, p11)

ICT as tool

In Chapter 1 we discussed the use of ICT as a tool, but a specific example to help develop inclusion is the use of mobile devices, such as hand-held computers. Although such tools (and other mobile devices) can be used with all pupils, Bauer and Ulrich (2002) found that the use of hand-held computers helped pupils with SEN to stay organised. They also found that the portability of the devices helped to reduce anxiety in children in Year 6 about knowing what they needed to do or losing papers. They further suggested that hand-held computers 'offer social support, as pupils can share programs with each other and send information to friends'. (Florian and Hegarty, 2004, p14) We could conjecture that the same may be true of more recent incarnations of hand-held devices, such as ipods.

ICT to communicate

Further ways in which ICT can help inclusion are that it can provide ways either to enhance, or even facilitate, communication through:

- Rich and engaging materials for learning – presentation using multi-modal and multi-media features of ICT
- New forms of writing (e.g. speech recognition)

- Augmentive and Alternative Communication (AAC): 'any means by which an individual can supplement or replace spoken communication. ' (Chiner, 2001, cited in Soan, 2004, p184)

All of the above provide opportunities to accommodate different learners, but challenges remain. Florian (2004, pp18–19) asserts that these may include the 'adaptations that may have to be made for learners to acquire or use the tools of technology. The opportunities lie in the way that technology can then be used to ameliorate the effects of what would otherwise create a barrier to learning or participation in an interactive activity'.

All of the above can help with differentiation leading to effective inclusion, leading to what we could call *inclusive differentiation*. In adopting this approach, there is, as with most ICT use, a commitment required from the teacher to ensure that not only are such options known about and considered, but, if they are adopted, that they are used effectively.

Perhaps the key idea in all of the above is that ICT use should not be regarded as the preserve of the more able, or indeed less able, or that of the teacher, but that as far as possible expectations of ICT use should be the same for *all* pupils.

ACTIVITY

Working in a group, or on your own, consider a topic you will be teaching and, using a suitable planning format, record how ICT could be used in different phases of the whole lesson (e.g introduction, main activities and plenary) to encourage inclusive differentiation. Part of this process would also include non-ICT resources and a key part of this activity is considering which is best to use on the basis of their 'fitness for purpose'. It may be that this would vary according to group, so some may use ICT and some may not. Obviously, if you know the class well you can target individual real groups, but,if you do not know a class well, you can still consider both ICT and non-ICT resources and decide on what may be appropriate to use in general terms.

E-safety

Finally, having made all other decisions about ICT use we need to consider e-safety, which may in turn lead to you to *not* use ICT after all! However, it is necessary to put concerns about e-safety in context to avoid such drastic measures. There is much hyperbole around this issue and, although Cranmer et al., (2009) suggest primary pupils' views of e-safety are at odds with official definitions, their views do reflect the reality of their everyday experiences. Cranmer et al., (2009, p140) continue to state that official policy should 'first focus on meaningful and grounded elements of children's everyday ICT experiences. Only when likely risks and dangers are established should discussion move towards messages of "risk" which focus on the more extreme concerns of stranger danger, paedophiles and other risks of the unknown "other"'.

Most primary schools will have in place a policy regarding e-safety, but they are likely to reflect official policies and perhaps not the reality of pupils' lives as discussed above. Despite this, however, they will all contain the key idea that e-safety is not about *restricting* children, but about *educating* them. In the first instance you may have to restrict them, but with the ultimate aim that they are educated to make judgements themselves. This is supported by the views of Ofsted (2010, p8), who state that 'in the best practice seen, pupils were helped, from a very early age, to assess the risk of accessing sites and therefore gradually to acquire skills which would help them adopt safe practices even when they were not supervised'. To develop this best practice, however, it is important that *you* are also educated in this area. We have already examined the concept of digital natives and immigrant and this is one area where this distinction can have a negative impact. As Becta (2007, p9) report:

> *For primary school children, certainly in the lower year groups, some of the risks might appear to be outside their level of ICT use. However, as the research shows, children engage with technology at an ever-younger age, and their knowledge and use of technological services, tools and devices can quickly outstrip that of their parents, carers and teachers.*

This concern is contextualised by figures from Ofcom (2010) which report that 73 per cent of UK households have access to the internet – with 71% having access to broadband if required. As suggested earlier in the chapter, this figure is already out of date and it seems unlikely that this access will decrease.

To help you in addressing e-safety, there are many primary school resources available to help (see 'Useful websites' below, p63). As such, it is not necessary here to cover this area in great depth, except to stress the importance on considering e-safety at all times ICT is used. What we do need to reflect on in broad terms is how to integrate e-safety in planning and preparation. We will do this under three headings:

- Filtering
- Moderation
- Supervision

Filtering

Most filtering will be done by school Firewalls which will block access to certain sites. You may also need to make your own 'filtering' judgment based on the age of the children you are teaching.

TIP

You need to be aware of this if you are planning to access sites for lessons as some Firewalls be very restrictive – just because you can access a site at home does not mean you can at school. In addition, just because you can access a site in one school, it does not follow that you can in all schools – for instance if you move schools, different counties have different levels of access. You always need to access the site from your classroom before using in lesson. This is an essential part of preparation for a lesson using internet resources.

Moderation

Moderation of web-based content is largely done reactively ('post-moderation' rather than 'pre-moderation') which, although helpful, is time consuming and cannot actually prevent inappropriate content. This does, however, ensure that pupils are free to contribute, for instance to blogs, freely and be 'empowered'. An alternative, and part of the educational process, is to peer-assess contributions before being published online or communicated electronically. In addition, with older children in the primary school, involving them in moderating sites can be a useful form of educating them about what is and is not acceptable.

Engaging parents

However good the education a school provides about e-safety, it is vital that both the school and you as a teacher engage with parents, especially in the area of socialising through electronic sources. This includes both obvious examples, such as social networking on internet sites, but also through perhaps less obvious ones such as gaming machines (for example Play station), which allow direct un-moderated communication between users if connected to the internet, which most can do using a wired or wireless connection.

Given the recent increase in internet access outlined by Ofcom (2010) above, it is also interesting to note that the same report stated that social networking now accounts for nearly a quarter (23 per cent) of all time spent online. It is suggested that as internet access increases even more, this statistic is also likely to increase both for adults and children. This is especially true when an increasing number of 'safe' networking sites (such as Club Penguin and Moshi Monsters) are specifically aimed at children, but mirror the characteristics of a chatroom. At present, use of social networking sites in schools is limited, but we do need to consider if this is actually beneficial. Sharples et al., (2008, p5) make an important point when they assert that:

> *Currently, most children are prevented from engaging in any social activity on the web at school. While this may remove the immediate danger to children and protect the school or local authority against lawsuits, it may also store up further problems for society at*

large. Now that most children have home access, safe behaviours are essential, but a strongly protected online environment at school may not provide the opportunity to learn these.

ACTIVITY

In groups, discuss if primary children should be allowed, and even encouraged, to use suitable social networking sites in school time? *If so, what are the benefits, both personally and in terms of the curriculum? If not, how can children learn safe behaviours?*

Supervision

Finally, in planning and preparing lessons we will consider the role of supervision and who will provide it. This is particularly important in early years settings and when you have support from another adults. In this context, it would not be appropriate to use a more able child (as in Vygotsky previously), as the 'supervisor' is being asked to make moral judgements, rather than to help scaffold the task. It is essential that the 'supervisor' shares both the school and your expectations on their role. In reality this will probably be a joint role in supporting learning and as 'moral guardian'. The role of the supervisor will be especially important with young children and those with particular needs which may affect their ability to interpret text, language, gesture or emotion.

If all else fails ...

Despite the best planning and preparation, on occasions things may go wrong. For instance, as Ofsted (2010) report, it is possible to begin searching for information on the Holocaust and end up on Nazi propaganda sites. Although all the precautions taken above should prevent it, Ofsted (2010, p9) conclude that

> *The most successful schools visited in terms of their e-safety ensured that pupils knew what to do when things went wrong. Three primary schools visited, for example, made sure that if pupils came across an unsuitable site they could activate a cartoon character which covered the screen; it meant that they did not have to look at the site and had the opportunity to tell an adult.*

Although the provision of such a character (or similar options) would be the responsibility of the school, it is your responsibility to ensure they know how and when to use it, and what to do next.

SUMMARY

In this chapter we have considered the role of ICT in planning and preparing lessons for pupils who have grown up in a world surrounded by technology and may be considered 'digital natives'. We have explored how classroom design can enable effective use of ICT in planning and preparing lessons, to ensure **all** pupils are included in activities. An important facet of this is how ICT can encourage 'e-inclusion'. Such an approach uses digital technologies as tools to explore and communicate ideas to minimise the problems that pupils with learning difficulties experience. In lessons, teachers are faced with a large and diverse range of learning styles and it is important that the full range of ICT resources are used effectively to engage different learner characteristics. Finally, it is important that all this work takes place in a safe 'e-environment', where pupils are educated aboutpotential dangers and know what to do when things went wrong.

In the next chapter we will examine the implications of the above in classroom teaching.

References

Abbot, C. (2007), *E-inclusion: learning difficulties and digital technologies*, London: Futurelab.

Beauchamp, G. (2011): 'Interactivity and ICT in the primary school: categories of learner interactions with and without ICT', *Technology, Pedagogy and Education*, 20(2), 175–190.

Becta (2007), *Signposts to safety: Teaching e-safety at Key Stages 1 and 2*, London: Becta.

Cranmer, S. (2006) 'Children and young people's uses of the Internet for homework', *Learning, Media and Technology*, 31(3), 301–15.

Cranmer, S., Selwyn, N. and Potter, J. (2009), 'Exploring primary pupils' experiences and understandings of 'e-safety', *Education and Information Technologies*, 14:127–42.

Egerton, J., Cook, J. and Stambolis, C. (undated), 'Developing a model of pedagogical best practice in the use of interactive whiteboards for children with autism and complex learning disabilities: implications for initial teacher training. **http://www.sunfield.org.uk/pdf/TDA_project.pdf** (Accessed 08.06.11)

Florian, L.(2004), 'Uses of technology that support pupils with special educational needs', in Florian, L. and Hegarty, J. (eds), *ICT and Special Educational Needs: A Tool for Inclusion*, Maidenhead: Open University Press. pp7–20.

Goswami, U. and Bryant, P. (2007), *Children's Cognitive Development and Learning* (Primary Review Research Survey 2/1a), Cambridge: University of Cambridge Faculty of Education.

Harrison, R. (1993), 'Disaffection and Access', in J. Calder (ed.) *Disaffection and Diversity. Overcoming Barriers to Adult Learning*, London: Falmer Press.

Higgins, S., Beauchamp, G. and Miller, D. (2007), 'Reviewing the literature on interactive whiteboards', *Learning, Media and Technology*, 32 (3), 213–25.

Jones, C.A. (2004), *Supporting Inclusion in the Early Years*, Maidenhead: Open University Press.

Kerry, T. and Kerry, C.A. (1997), 'Differentiation: teachers' views of the usefulness of recommended strategies in helping the more able pupils in primary and secondary classrooms', *Educational Studies*, 23(3), pp439–57.

Kerawalla, L. and Crook, C, (2002), 'Children's computer use at home and at school: context and continuity', *British Educational Research Journal*, 28(6), pp751–71.

Ofsted (2010), *The safe use of new technologies*, Manchester: Ofsted.

Pearson, M. and Somekh, B. (2003) 'Concept-mapping as a research tool: a study of primary children's representations of information and communication technologies (ICT)', *Education and Information Technologies* 8(1), pp5–22.

Lewis, L., Trushell, J. and Woods, P. (2005), 'Effects of ICT group work on interactions and social acceptance of a primary pupil with Asperger's Syndrome', *British Journal of Educational Technology*, 36(5), pp739–55.

Means, B. (ed.) (1994), *Technology and Education Reform: The Reality Behind the Promise*, San Francisco, CA: Josssey-Bass.

Medwell, J. (2007), *Successful Teaching Placement: Primary and Early Years*, Exeter: Learning Matters.

Miller, D., Glover, D. and Averis, D. (2004), 'A worthwhile investment? the interactive whiteboard and the teaching of mathematics', Keele: Keele University [online at: **http://www.keele.ac.uk/depts/ed/iaw** accessed: 28.3.08]

OECD (2001), *Understanding The Digital Divide*, Paris: OECD.

Ofcom (2010) Communications Market Report (Online at **http://stakeholders.ofcom.org.uk/market-data-research/market-data/communications-market-reports/cmr10/uk/** accessed 08.06.11)

Rahamin, L. (2004), 'From integration to inclusion: using ICT to support learners with special educational needs in the ordinary classroom', in Florian, L. and Hegarty, J., (eds) *ICT and Special Educational Needs: A Tool for Inclusion*, Maidenhead: Open University Press, pp35–45.

Selwyn, N., Boraschi, D. and Özkula, S.M. (2009), 'Drawing digital pictures: an investigation of primary pupils' representations of ICT and schools', *British Educational Research Journal*, 35(6), pp909–28.

Selwyn, N., Potter, J. and Cranmer, S. (2009), 'Primary pupils' use of information and communication technologies at school and home', *British Journal of Educational Technology*, 40(5), pp919–32.

Selwyn, N., Gorard, S. and Furlong, J. 'Adults' use of ICTs for learning: reducing or increasing educational inequalities?' *Journal of Vocational Education and Training*, Volume 56, Number 2, 2004, pp269–90.

Sharp, C. (2006), 'Becoming a research-engaged school: using whiteboards and ICT', *Practical Research for Education* [NFER], 35 (May), 56–61 [online at: **www.pre-online.co.uk**; accessed: 29.05.2011]

Sharples, M., Graber, R., Harrison, C. and Logan, K. (2008), *E-safety and Web 2.0 technologies for Learning at Key Stages 3 and 4*, Coventry: BECTA.

Smeets, E. and Mooij, T. (2001), 'Pupil-centred learning, ICT, and teacher behaviour: observations in educational practice', *British Journal of Educational Technology*, 32(40), pp403–17.

Soan, S. (ed.) (2004), *Additional Educational Needs: Inclusive Approaches to Teaching*, London: David Fulton.

Thomas, G., Walker, D. and Webb, J. (2005), 'Inclusive education: the ideals and the practice', in Topping, K. and Maloney, S. (eds), *The RoutledgeFalmer Reader in Inclusive Education*, London: Routledge, pp17–28.

Thomas, G. and Vaughan, M. (2004), *Inclusive Education: Reading and Reflections*, Maidenhead: Open University Press.

Westwood, P. (2005), 'Adapting Curriculum and Instruction', in Topping, K. and Maloney, S. (eds), *The RoutledgeFalmer Reader in Inclusive Education*, London: Routledge. pp145–159.

Woolfson, L.M. (2011), *Educational Psychology: The Impact of Psychological Research on Education*, London: Pearson.

Further reading

Becta (2007) *Signposts to safety: Teaching e-safety at Key Stages 1 and 2*. London: Becta. *As well as covering the area of e-safety in general this resource also includes advice on 'Embedding e-safety issues into the curriculum at Key Stages 1 and 2.*

Egerton, J., Cook, J. and Stambolis, C. (undated), 'Developing a model of pedagogical best practice in the use of interactive whiteboards for children with autism and complex learning disabilities: implications for initial teacher training (Training and Development Agency for Schools R&D Award (SEN) 2), Sunfield Research. (Accessed from **http://tinyurl.com/4x5yfqw**) *A useful summary of research literature on the interactive whiteboard, but more importantly a guide to how to use the IWB a range of learning disabilities.*

Florian, L. and Hegarty, J. (eds), (2004) ICT and special educational needs: a tool for inclusion, Maidenhead: Open University Press. *An edited collection covering a range of issues relating to ICT and SEN.*

Ofsted (2010), *The safe use of new technologies*, Manchester: Ofsted.

Useful websites

E-safety

Child Exploitation and Online Protection Centre: **http://ceop.police.uk/** *Information for teachers and pupils from the UK police.*

Childnet: **http://www.childnet-int.org/kia/primary/teachers.aspx**

CHAPTER 5 ICT in the Early Years

In this chapter we will examine the place of ICT in the particular context of Early Years (EY) teaching. We will consider how the unique pedagogy of this age range can influence the use of ICT and provide examples of what this may look like in action.

The Early Years context

> *ICT [in the EY] is not just a computer with Early Years software installed. ICT is anything where you can press a button and make something happen, the beginnings of children understanding that technology requires programming and that they can be in control of making things happen.*
>
> **(http://tinyurl.com/3c864xz)**

In recent years, Early Years (EY) education has been transformed by development such as Foundation Stage in England, the Foundation Phase in Wales – which introduced one 'key stage' from age 3–7 years – and the view in Scotland of all learning from 3–18 being one continuum – see more below. At the same time, advances in technology have changed the way people live and interact, in educational settings and at home. From a very early age children are exposed to an increasingly sophisticated array of technology to use in work and, more importantly for this chapter, play. Marsh et al., (2005, p5) undertook a large study of parents, carers and early years practitioners and concluded that 'young children are immersed in practices relating to popular culture, media and new technologies from birth. They are growing up in a digital world and develop a wide range of skills, knowledge and understanding of this world from birth'. More recently, in a review of research into ICT in the early years, Aubrey and Dahl (2008, p4) found evidence that

> *… most young children aged from birth to five years are growing up in media-rich digital environments in which they engage actively from a very early age. Family members are positive about this and actively promote the use of new technologies through on-going social-cultural practices of the home. They welcome ICT education outside the home and believe that it should be included in the curriculum from the earliest days. Young children are confident with new technologies and are very willing to explore new gadgets that they have not encountered before.*

This openness to explore, or play, with new technologies is something that teachers need to both embrace and facilitate. For this reason, this chapter (unlike others) will also include some classroom activities to exemplify how ICT may be used in this context. Although teachers may be worried by new technologies, or about damaging expensive equipment, we need to be sure that this is not transmitted to young children, or that other obstacles are not put in the ways of their natural curiosity or willingness to explore new technologies. Potential obstacles could include:

- Robustness of hardware – little hands can cause big damage!
- Size of hardware – especially if intended to be held in small hands
- Degree of fine motor skills needed to use/control equipment
- Use of language (spoken instructions on websites) or writing (or other symbols, including letters) that are not developmentally appropriate

ACTIVITY

Consider ICT equipment in a classroom you know well and consider how it was chosen in view of the above and the resultant advantages or disadvantages of each.

Although these factors will have already been considered for existing equipment when it was purchased, this does not mean that you should ignore the potential obstacles above when planning learning experiences. Within an early setting there is a wide range of levels of development and by considering these factors you are also thinking about issues of differentiation with learners of the same age.

In addition to functioning ICT equipment, Morgan and Siraj-Blatchford (2009) point out the importance of also having 'pretend' technological devices to use alongside other play equipment. They suggest that

> *ICT education may be supported through the inclusion of ICT props such as 'point of sale' cash registers and bar code scanners, pretend (or working) telephones and computer equipment. Often the props can be made in collaboration with the children developing a play area for a particular topic such as 'At the Vets', 'Going to the Dentist', A Travel Agency or a 'Supermarket' etc. Role projects of this kind are often supported by visits to the appropriate vetinary surgery, travel agents or supermarket. (p15)*

As part of these visits pupils will also see functioning ICT versions of their own play equipment; indeed this could be part of an ICT walk below. But, back in the classroom, ICT equipment is part of pupils' everyday life, so should be part of their everyday play.

CLASSROOM IDEA:

ICT walk

ICT Equipment: digital voice recorders, video cameras, and digital camera

Features of ICT:

Speed

Automation

Interactivity

Take children on a walk, first of all around the classroom, then around the school and even beyond – such as a visit above. Make a list of all ICT that you see. *Why not use ICT (digital voice recorders, video cameras, digital cameras) to make the list?* The discussion about what is ICT and what is not is a central part of this activity. Also, reviewing the list(s) afterwards (using IWB, on PC/laptop or paper) can be useful in highlighting the wide range of both ICT equipment we rely on, but also other things that depend on them (street light, traffic lights ...). This could be done as a group activity and each group reports back to the class or other groups. This can also link to displays and setting up activity areas and so on.

In addition to these pragmatic issues, the Developmentally Appropriate Technology in Early Childhood Education (DATEC) project suggested there are seven general principles for 'determining the effectiveness of ICT applications – or uses of ICT – in the early years, to help practitioners provide the best possible experiences. They are:

1. ensure an educational purpose
2. encourage collaboration
3. integrate with other aspects of curriculum
4. ensure the child is in control
5. choose applications that are transparent – their functions should be clearly defined and intuitive
6. avoid applications containing violence or stereotyping
7. be aware of health and safety issues*

Parental involvement should also go hand-in-hand with these'.

(http://www.datec.org.uk/datecfrm1.htm).

*Since these principles were developed it is now necessary to amend the latter to include e-safety – see Chapter 4.

The first of these principles should not be taken to mean that ICT resources not aimed specifically at the education market should be ignored. It does, however, mean that applications 'should be educational in nature and this effectively excludes all those applications where clear learning aims cannot be identified'. (Siraj-Blatchford and

Whitebread, 2003, p8) We have already considered the importance of collaboration (dialogic and interactive teaching), the child being in control (co-constructor of knowledge) and health and safety issues/e-safety. But, the third principle is vital in the context of early years education, where developing the whole child is considered to be important and 'learning is holistic and interconnected. The young child does not separate experiences into different compartments'. (Fisher, 2002, p44) In this context, ICT is not a separate 'subject', but contributes to all areas of learning. Having said this, the EYFS does outline a progression in ICT use and skills which requires that from birth, pupils are expected to show interest in 'toys and resources that incorporate technology', progressing through to 'showing interest in toys with buttons and flaps', before gaining 'basic skills in turning on and operating some ICT equipment' and completing a 'simple program on a computer' and using ICT 'to perform simple functions'. (DCFS, 2008, pp83–84)

CLASSROOM IDEA:

Our Talking book – Our class

Features of ICT:

Speed

Automation

Capacity

Range

Provisionality

Interactivity

ICT Equipment: digital cameras, interactive whiteboard, computer, software package to create pages (e.g. ActivStudio or Notebook, even PowerPoint), imagination and voice recorder (e.g. built in to computer or digital voice recorder or mobile phone)

Children take digital photographs of each other. These could be in their own clothes or fancy dress depending on the story. For instance, one picture could be 'My name is ...' in normal clothes and the next could be 'I want to be a ...' dressed up in relevant clothes. Make pages by inserting pictures, then make voice recordings of them saying the text above (or whatever else they want to say!). When complete show to the class but also share with other classes – and even keep for next year to show as an example, for staff training session or parent's evening.

Extension:

Text can be added with children helping as their ICT skill level allows. You could use a keyboard or scan in their writing (e.g. their name) if appropriate.

This type of activity can also work with different title such as 'We can count / We speak Welsh/ French ...'.

The 'curriculum' context

Having said that ICT should be used in all areas of learning, this aim is unfortunately set in the context of the regulation of what is taught in most educational settings. The extent of the regulation can change fundamentally with new governments and the context in which EY settings work is complex and evolving. There is an inevitable tension between a child-centred approach, where each child is an individual with their own specific needs, and the political imperative to account for public money by monitoring and raising 'standards'. The latter has resulted in various attempts to formalise what, and even how, children learn. At the time of writing this chapter, the UK has several 'frameworks' (curricula), which have been influenced to greater or lesser degrees by the EY pedagogy from various other countries, notably Scandinavia and New Zealand. Although a direct match of the EY curricula is difficult, table 5.1 below attempts to give a current overview to show both common themes and diversity, particularly in the age range they apply to.

Table 5.1 Comparison of UK EY curricula contexts

England:	**Wales:**	**Scotland:**
Foundation Stage Early Learning Goals (3–5 years)	Foundation Phase Areas of Learning (3–7 years)	Curriculum for Excellence Experiences and outcomes (3–15 [18] years)
6 areas	7 areas	8 areas
Personal, Social and Emotional Development	Personal and Social Development, Well-Being and Cultural Diversity	Religious and moral education
Communication, Language and Literacy	Language, Literacy and Communication Skills	Languages – including 'Literacy and English', 'classical' and Gaelic
	Welsh Language Development*	
Problem Solving, Reasoning and Numeracy	Mathematical Development	Mathematics
Knowledge and Understanding of the World	Knowledge and Understanding of the World	Sciences
Physical Development	Physical Development	Health and wellbeing
Creative Development	Creative Development	Expressive arts
		Social studies
		Technologies
http://tinyurl.com/3bdrjzo	**http://tinyurl.com/3dnnemh**	**http://tinyurl.com/6nd568**

* This relates to English-medium schools, where the Welsh language is taught as a second language in all primary schools in Wales.

What is immediately obvious is the 'bigger picture' in which EY education resides. In England, it remains separate from Key Stage 1 (KS1) and above (where currently a subject-based framework is introduced), whilst in Scotland and Wales EY education is firmly integrated into that of older age groups. There is not space here to discuss this further, but you may wish to consider the implications of this and the view it reflects of how children learn. (See also Palaiologou et al., 2010 in further reading below.)

While none of the above may be called a curriculum in all senses of the word, it will be easiest to use this term for the remainder of this chapter to describe the generic frameworks for this stage of education. All of these curricula have ICT in them, but the intention above is that it should pervade all areas. In the English EYFS, the most direct mention of ICT comes in Knowledge and Understanding of the World which states that children should be supported 'in using a range of ICT to include cameras, photocopiers, CD players, tape recorders and programmable toys in addition to computers'. The guidance in Wales for the Foundation Phase is more explicit and echoes the child-centred learning ethos of ETY learning discussed above:

> *ICT should be holistic and integral across the curriculum. Children's ICT skills, knowledge and understanding should be developed through a range of experiences that involve them (i) finding and developing information and ideas, (ii) creating and presenting information and ideas.*
>
> *Children's progression in ICT capability should be observed with an understanding of child development and the stages children move through. Children should be given opportunities to develop their skills using a wide range of equipment and software.*
>
> **(DCELLS, 2008, p11)**

The Scottish curriculum provides a helpful, and child-centred, categorisation below, which can also help us to identify what skills and resources we need to provide for young children:

- I explore software and use what I learn to solve problems and present my ideas, thoughts, or information.
- I enjoy exploring and using technologies to communicate with others within and beyond my place of learning.
- I enjoy taking photographs or recording sound and images to represent my experiences and the world around me.

(http://tinyurl.com/3ebp88e)

From this we can see that a range of ICT equipment, functioning and not functioning (for role play situations), is needed. As well as laptop and handheld computers (and touch screen devices such as ipad) and age-specific software, EY settings also need a variety of ICT resources that could include:

- Digital cameras/video recorders (still images and movies)
- Good internet connection – access to email
- microphones (or digital recorders – including on portable devices)
- programmable toys
- remote control toys
- walkie-talkies
- electronic microscopes

- DVDs
- dance mats / musical devices (e.g. keyboards)
- overhead projector
- IWBs.

As technology advances, so will the length of this list. By the time you read this you may be thinking, 'why is … not included?'. For all of these pieces of equipment, young children will need some explicit ICT skills to use them effectively, but these can be taught as required in context of topics. Indeed, with support from classroom assistants or other children who can work them, young children should not be restricted by a lack of 'technical' or IT skill. Indeed, young children will pick up many skills informally from observing others, as they do in their homes by watching older siblings or parents. This is not to suggest that you do not need to consider teaching relevant skills, but you should not underestimate what children are able to achieve by taking part in activities with others.

CLASSROOM IDEA:

Bear hunt (or any suitable story involving moving from place to place)

Features of ICT:

Automation

Interactivity

ICT Equipment: **floor robot and 'maps'**

After hearing a story (such as the 'Bear Hunt') children develop a map on large pieces of paper of the places in the story using pens, paint or any other suitable medium (creative development). When they are ready children can work in pairs or small groups to control the programmable toy/ floor robot as it moves from place to place on the map. (see example **http://tinyurl.com/3shcl8q**)

Extension: children can develop new maps and then make the story to go with them. These can be developed as stories, short plays (videoed) or even pod casts as well as for use with floor robots / programmable toys. Alternatively, children could build a physical maze using outdoor equipment that the robots have to navigate.

Problem-solving, creativity and 'playful' use of ICT

We have already established that young children are not afraid to 'play' and be creative with ICT in general. Some types of ICT aim to specifically exploit this by using the unique features of ICT we have examined in earlier chapters. This is particularly true of games and simulations. Whitebread (2006) outlines three characteristics of these which research suggest are helpful in helping young children understand and mentally 'represent' problems they are trying to solve:

1. Problems are embedded in 'meaningful contexts' – e.g. adventure stories where you help the characters overcome a series of challenges rather than the child being faced with these same challenges in isolation without a context – the latter being what Whitebread (2006, p87) labels 'arid and obviously artificial problems of the 'if two men can dig a hole in three days' variety'.
2. Problems are simplified or 'cleaned up' to help young children see the significant features – in the same way we simplify the way we talk to younger children.
3. The same kinds of problems are posed in a variety of different contexts.

Whitebread (2006, p93) concludes that 'well constructed adventure games and simulations provide a wealth of opportunities for children to practise the skills of reasoning, hypothesis testing and decisions making'. These games and simulations can be found on CD-ROMs, specific software programs and increasingly on websites. Although not all of the latter are aimed at the education market specifically, they can have a valid use in educational settings if carefully used and monitored. Indeed, some of these 'collaborative' internet games can actually allow children to collaborate in problem solving with others in different classes, schools or even countries.

CLASSROOM IDEA:

Our outdoor play area

ICT Equipment: video or sound recorders, IWB or computer with sound capability

Features of ICT:

Speed

Automation

Range

Provisionality (taking and discarding of photos)

Interactivity

Provisionality: As well as using features such as undo and redo on the IWB, provisionality also applies to other ICT equipment, such as the taking and deleting of photographs and the digital camera – see below.

Although this is about the outdoor area the activity can be repeated in other contexts, such as 'My favourite place' (in school). The focus of the activity is to produce material for a new page on the school website. (*If you search the internet for 'Our outdoor play area' you will find some examples but few contain materials by pupils – the vocabulary is a giveaway – and limited use of ICT except for digital pictures.)* The pupils are asked to take pictures of their favourite part of the outdoor play area, record thoughts (using a variety of media) on why they like it and what they do there. The activity takes place in small groups as part of a rotation of activities and the group is supported by an adult helper – but only in using equipment if they choose to use it. After material is collected the class discuss what they would like to use by viewing on the IWB or other suitable medium. The end product is uploaded to the school website.

Research tip: Mosaic approach

As many teachers undertake research of some kind, even if not for an academic qualification, we will briefly consider the advantages of using ICT in the Mosaic Approach, as the activity outlined above could form part of such the piece of research. Clark (2010) provides more details of the Mosaic approach, but in essence it uses a mixture of traditional (observation and interview) and other techniques (or pieces) to build a picture from a variety of sources and individuals. It is particularly useful for finding the views of pupils in EY settings – but could be used with all ages including adults. The 'pieces' of the mosaic are:

- Observation
- Interviews
- Book making
- Tours
- Slide shows
- Map making

Each technique/piece is intended to contribute to the whole picture/mosaic, but there is no reason why each should not be used separately – such as in 'Our outdoor play area'. Of particular interest to us is how ICT can contribute. In the context of traditional techniques such as observations and interviews, there is an obvious role for video and audio recording. What is perhaps of more interest is how ICT can contribute to the other 'pieces'.

Book making provides pupils with an opportunity to use photography to take photographs of important things in their environment to compile them into a book. Only one child at a time uses the camera, but others may accompany the photographer, including the adult in a passive role – in other words making sure not to suggest what is to be photographed. Any device can be used to take the pictures, but it may be best to use digital cameras designed for use with EY pupils. The aspect of provisionality we have discussed above means that children can take, retake and delete as many photographs as the capacity of the camera will allow. (This is a great advantage over disposable cameras, which contain a finite amount of film.) The digital nature of these photographs

(*continued*)

also means that compiling a book, or indeed adding them to a slide show, is an easy task. When compiling the book, it is also easy to view the pictures using a variety of tools.

Tours encourage pupils to show adults around their environment, indicating what is important to them. An individual, pairs or small groups, can conduct these tours. The role of the 'researcher' in the process is as an interested adult. Clark (2010, p37) suggests that 'the use of child-led tours privileges the way that young children communicate in active, visual ways. This method does not rely on verbal communication as children can point out features, but rich conversations may be triggered by children walking through their environment'. Although Clark suggests the researcher takes field notes, it may also be possible, with the advent of very small cameras, to also use video recordings to capture gesture, emotion and vocabulary.

Slide shows can be used to show not only pictures taken by the pupils, but also those of other settings. Early work in this area used slide projectors, but the ability of an IWB to allow a number of pupils to view the same image, or to show on suitable television screens, has changed the nature of this work, if not the name. The role of the researcher is to monitor the actions of the children as they interact with the images and record any resulting conversations.

Map making can range in sophistication from young children's interpretations of their environment in any form, through to more sophisticated versions using ICT tools. The intention of creating the maps, which can hold information about both the past and present, is to record both remembered events and geographical locations. ICT also has a role in recording (for example, by scanning work) and sharing the work of others. The main function of the map is to enable them record significant places, and 'this is not map making in order to gain accurate topographical records'. (Clark, 2010, p40)

As already stated, although the intention is to create an overall picture made up of many pieces, each technique may also be valuable to teachers as a separate activity in gaining evidence of how children feel about their environment and about each other. Even if not used for research purposes, such information is valid in records of achievement or pupil profiles.

When to use ICT in the EY?

With such a wealth of resources available, it is important to consider *when* they can be used. All such decisions need to be focused on exploiting the features of ICT to best effect and how this contributes to achieving the desired learning outcome. Many of these uses of ICT will take the form of interactions between pupil and ICT, or between pupils through ICT. Based on a small scale case study of literacy activities in an American kindergarten Labbo et al., (2000) suggest that three kinds of interactions with ICT that could be effective in early years settings:

1. brief targeted moments – consist of activities that take 5 to 10 minutes to complete.
2. spur-of-the-moment ideas – usually consist of child-initiated, spontaneous activities that can be accomplished with little prior planning and that make use of available materials.
3. thematically linked activities – carefully planned, multi-layered activities that involve multiple opportunities to learn key concepts in various ways.

(http://www.readingonline.org/electronic/labbo/)

Within these interactions, and others besides, teachers need to make decisions about what equipment to use. Kennington and Meaton (2009) remind us that the most important factor is not the equipment, but the way that it is used. They also rightly suggest that it is not always the most expensive piece of equipment that is the best. They give the example of 'talking tins', which are smallplastic 'discs' (8cm diameter and 2cm deep) that can record sound (from 10 seconds to 40 seconds and costing from £3 to £8 at the time of writing) and play back and record at the press of a button. They also have a built-in magnet which means they can be attached to suitable metal objects or surfaces – although there are also straps to attach to other things. **(http://tinyurl.com/q2fxvz)**

These simple devices, and whatever replaces them as technology advances, have many uses for both pupils and teachers. Like other ICT resources which do the same thing,these devices do not get bored of saying the same thing time and again. They can be re-recorded easily (but can also be locked to prevent loss of recording), and are easy to carry and operate. A few examples of their use are below, all with educational purposes, but you could easily think of more:

- Pupils draw pictures of themselves and put on wall. They record their name and something about themselves on 'tin' and stick this to the wall with a 'press me' or similar pictorial label;
- Teacher places the tins around the outdoor play area with instructions of where to go next on a treasure trail;
- Teacher places tins around school hall with instructions for activities (e.g. jump in the air three times);
- Teacher places the tin next to an activity with no adult support as reminder of what to do;
- Teacher puts next to objects with recordings of a language being learned (e.g. Welsh) or English for learners.

CLASSROOM IDEA:

Message in a (electronic) bottle

ICT Equipment: video or sound recorders, IWB or computer with sound capability, clip art of bottles or digital pictures, suitable background.

Features of ICT:

According to your ICT confidence you can start this activity in any way but the key idea is the message has washed up on shore. One easy way is to use an image similar to the first picture above on a PowerPoint slide with waves sound effects. You can then have another image on the next slide and include your own message and picture, for example a picture of a teddy and a message asking for help finding it – you can also record the speech and click on it (or auto play) to read the text for those who may find it hard. Many activities could follow this – e.g. find a hidden teddy, plan a journey to find him, ...

Alternatively, you could just use the first slide (using the features of ICT – sound, automation ...) and then produce 'the actual bottle' and open with the children.

ICT and personal confidence

In addition to the confidence that ICT can give to pupils by presenting their written work in a highly professional manner, instead of their emerging handwriting, it can also be used to give pupils a voice. This voice can be through a variety of formats, such as photography or music, but can also encourage pupils to use their real voice in new ways. James and Cane (2009) report a range of instances including:

- using a remote controlled car encourage a pupil to extend his sentences;
- using a karaoke machine encouraged a withdrawn three-year-old to sing, then continue to talk to the class through the system;
- the use of a voice changer device encouraged a pupil who was self-conscious about his accent to talk to peers.

From this we can see that ICT can help young children to find a variety of voices that can encourage communication not only with other pupils but also with teachers.

SUMMARY

From all of the above, we may conclude that ICT use should form part of a heuristic learning experience, with play being central to learning using both functioning and non-functioning ICT resources. In this sense, ICT can be the subject of play, a tool for play or a method of stimulating play. Although some explicit teaching of skills will be required, pupils are also able to learn from each other, by observing the teacher and by using ICT resourcesto gain access to a range of different voices to facilitate and encourage communication.

References

Aubrey, C. and Dahl, S. (2008), *A review of the evidence on the use of ICT in the Early Years Foundation Stag*, Coventry: Becta.

Clark, A. (2010), *Transforming Children's Spaces: Children and Adult's Participation in Designing Learning Environments*, London: Routledge.

DCELLS (2008), *Framework for Children's Learning for 3 to 7-year-olds in Wales*, Cardiff: WAG.

DCFS (2008), *Practice Guidance for the Early Years Foundation Stage*, Annesley: DCFS Publications.

Fisher, J. (2002), *Starting from the Child* (2nd edition), Maidenhead: Open University Press.

James. K. and Cane, C. (2009), 'Giving, children a voice by using ICT', in in Price, H. (ed) *The Really Useful Book of ICT in the Early Years*, London: Routledge, pp53–68.

Kennington, L. and Meaton, J. (2009), in Price, H. (ed.), *The Really Useful Book of ICT in the Early Years*, London: Routledge, pp4–24.

Labbo, L. and Sprague, L., with Montero, M.K. and Font, G. (2000), **http://www.readingonline.org/electronic/labbo/**(Accessed on */////*)

Marsh, J., Brooks, G., Hughes, J., Ritchie, L., Roberts, S. and Wright, K. (2005) Digital beginnings: Young children's use of popular culture, media and new technologies. University of Sheffield: Literacy Research Centre

Morgan, Al. and Siraj-Blatchford, I. (2009), *Using ICT in the Early Years: Parents and Practitioners in Partnership*, London: Practical Pre-School Books.

Siraj-Blatchford, I., and Whitebread, D. (2003) *Supporting ICT in the Early Years*, Maidenhead: Open University Press.

Whitebread (2006), 'Creativity, problem-solving and playful uses of technology: games and simulations in the early years', in Hayes, M. and Whitebread, D. (eds) *ICT in the Early* Years, Maidenhead: Open University Press.

Further reading

Palaiologou, I., Walsh, G., Dunphy, E., Lyle, S. and Thomas-Williams, J. (2010), 'The National, Picture' in Palaiologou, I. (ed) *The Early Years Foundation Stage: Theory and Practice*, London: Sage, pp19–37s.

Useful websites

ICT in the Early years: **http://ictearlyyears.e2bn.org/index.php** Website of Homerton Children's Centre with wide resources to explore how ICT can be used in the EYFS. The site has areas covering planning, resources and a gallery of images showing ICT in action.

ICT and English in Key Stage 1 and 2

In this chapter we will examine how ICT has changed the conventional notion of Literacy and consider the impact of this in the classroom. The potential use of ICT in the areas of Speaking and Listening, Reading and Writing are analysed taking account of a range of new literacies.

Ideas in this chapter, and the next, will not be tied to age-related progression, such as Key Stages 1 and 2, but rather consider the progression in, and of, ideas. This is important because, as we saw in Chapter 2, ideas do not develop in strict accordance with age.

Literacy

As we have seen in earlier chapters, advances in ICT lead to a situation where new skills are needed both by teachers and learners. This may be especially true in the area of literacy, where learners are required to move beyond traditional printed texts and even the use of text itself. Brindley (2000, p14) suggests that literacy 'is the broader canvas. ICT is the medium of access and construction'. Using this 'medium' can present both technical and philosophical challenges. Technical challenges can come from new techniques to be mastered (such as hyperlinks), but some also come from changes in attitude in those that contribute to the fast growing amount of information available to pupils – and indeed teachers. One of the most significant is the move away from 'filter then publish' to 'publish then filter' by creators of digital content. (Shirky, 2008 cited in Hellen, 2011, p108) The result of this, and other factors, is that new key skills are needed in relation to ICT and English, which will help gain skills in both access and construction. Rudd and Tyldesley (2006) suggest these include:

- **The ability to find information** – learners no longer have a conventional index, table of contents or page numbers. Instead they have to learn to navigate electronic texts, and teachers need to equip them to recognise signposts and clues.
- **The ability to develop critical thinking and evaluate** – when we pick up a book or a letter we have learned to make some judgements about reliability and authority. Electronic Media do not always give the same clues. The validity of a text from a respectable publisher offers some assurance of quality, whereas the website can be published by anybody.

- **The ability to re-present information in different ways for different audiences** – new media literacy relies heavily on the skill of reading. It is important, however, that children are taught to produce text as authors, web designers or multimedia creators.
- **The ability to use new media as a creative space** – we have seen above some examples of how new media can lead to creativity in a way that is simply not possible without ICT.

In order to learn these skills across the curriculum, there is a need to teach specific skills in advance of them being needed (planning ahead in ICT lessons), but also it could be argued that this need will be greater in the earlier years of the primary school. This does not mean that pupils should be underestimated (young children can still edit video for example), but that they need to learn relevant skills at a level appropriate to their maturational and intellectual development – for instance, lack of fine motor control may prevent a particular piece of equipment being used effectively. As well as practical skills, pupils also need to be able to interpret a range of new media and understand how it can influence them. There is evidence from primary schools in Hong Kong and other countries that media education, as a discrete area of learning, can be beneficial in enabling primary pupils to construct and interpret a range of media (Cheung, 2005).

In the new world of technology, many pieces of equipment and software do not rely on text / reading, but rather use icons or images to convey information and even emotions. This means that pupils can often work ahead of their conventional reading age. Perhaps a helpful way of thinking is to consider each piece of software and hardware you are going to use and work out a progression sequence for each using relevant headings such as reading, writing, motor control and technical skills. You may want to 'audit' the ICT skills of children (e.g. with a digital camera – can they take picture, focus, review pictures, transfer to computer and so on) before you start working with them, as you would for any other area of the curriculum. Most teachers would not start teaching a topic unless they had assessed what children already know; why should ICT be any different? This would also help you in setting challenging, and individual, targets for each child.

Bennett et al., (2007) provide a model of ICT capability (see Figure 6.1), which shows how pupils develop growing independence based on the acquisition of skill, routines, techniques and key ideas of ICT. They suggest that the shape of the cone represents 'both the progression of activities ... [and] the numerical relationships between the elements of capability e.g. the key ideas of ICT are relatively few in number compared to the number of basic skills that must be learned'. (Bennett et al., 2007, p21) As we have seen above, considering where the pupil starts in the spiral is important to ensure challenge. In addition, however, considering such a model also reminds you that for each lesson or topic you teach you may have to start at the bottom with new skills before pupils can work independently. This applies even in Year 6 if the pupils are mastering a new piece of equipment or software. In planning lessons, an easy mistake is to equate older children automatically with independence in one area, just because they have it in another. This applies both within ICT as a subject and in applying it in other areas of the curriculum.

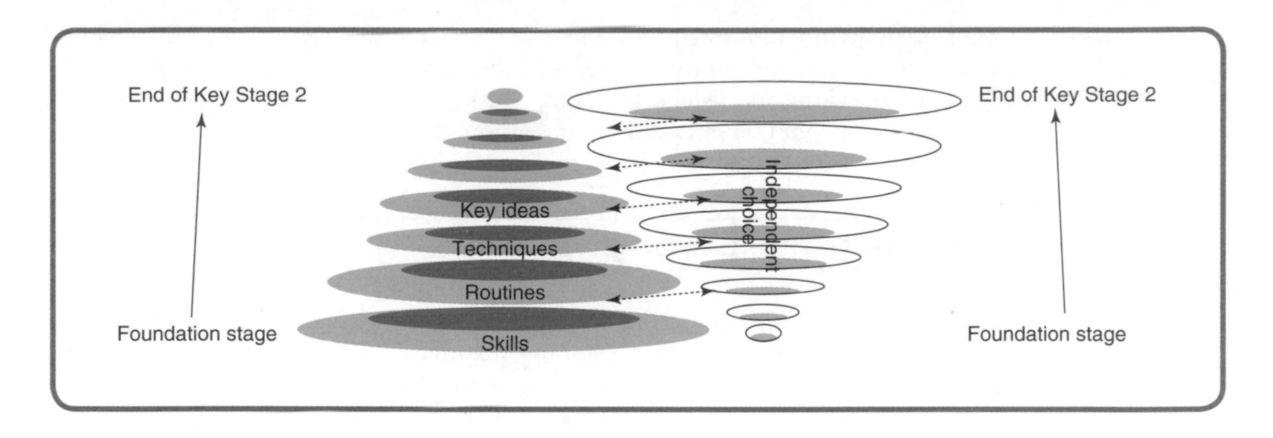

Figure 6.1 A model of ICT capability — the global level

All of the above does not mean that 'traditional' skills like reading and writing are not important, but in our new media world they

> *are not restricted to the mere coding and decoding of text, rather they are being used to describe the processes of extracting meaning from, and recording and presenting your own meaning through, the full range of media. This would include the ability to manipulate the basic tools required to create and access these media, just as holding a pen, forming letters and turning pages are part of text-based literacy. The end-products of literacy can range from a note to the milkman, to a hypertext on the Romans to a feature film. The common thread is that author a group of authors have an idea or set of ideas which they wish to present to an audience. (McFarlane, 2000, p19)*

Such an approach would use many modes of communication (see *Multimodal*), including visual representation, sound, movement, gesture and language, although the value of individual modes made vary between countries and cultures. What does not vary, however, is that in any single communicational event, different modes will be combined, with one or more becoming more prominent depending on the person communicating, the message they are trying to give and their intended audience. In this situation, 'meaning is made through complex interactions between the different modes' (Sutherland et al., 2009, p118) and no communication is 'monomodal' (Kress and Jewitt, 2008). One implication of such views is that we must challenge 'the implicit assumption that speech and writing are always central and sufficient for learning'. (Kress and Jewitt, 2008, p2) Such an assertion does not in any way imply that speech and writing are not vital for education, but it does suggest that we should consider carefully their position in a constantly evolving world of technology. In this consideration, we may conclude that pupils need to be equipped to view language as a 'metamode' (Matthewman, 2009) that enables them to access the meanings of a wide variety of texts, images, sounds and information within their cultural context, both in terms of the school setting and wider society. ICT is the source of some of these modes, but it also provides access to others, as well as a means of raising and answering questions through shared endeavour – more on this to follow below.

Unfortunately, in educational terms we have to frame this argument in the slightly less esoteric context of the requirements of a national curriculum, which at present focuses on speaking and listening, reading and writing, which we will now consider in turn as they would be important even without a National Curriculum.

Speaking and listening

There has been much research in recent years in the United Kingdom (UK) that explores how ICT contributes to developing talk in the classroom. This is particularly true when using the interactive whiteboard, especially in the context of whole-class teaching. We have already briefly discussed dialogic teaching (see Chapter 2) but it is now possible to explore this and other concepts in relations to ICT in more detail, with a special emphasis on the role of the IWB.

Central to this exploration are three components of the dialogic approach outlined by Warwick, Hennessy and Mercer (2011):

- Dialogue should support the co-construction of knowledge and understanding;
- Dialogue should make reasoning explicit; and
- Dialogue should be cumulative.

The authors report that 'cumulative' talk can be interpreted in different ways, but conclude that 'whole-class dialogue should allow the participants to orientate themselves to other perspectives and to evaluate their own ideas and solutions against others' statements and propositions'. (Warwick, Hennessy and Mercer, 2011, p307) In this context, it is important to note that 'dialogue' can include spoken language, but also includes other modes of communication facilitated by the IWB, such as annotating, drawing, sorting and manipulating images. This is important, as it allows pupils who may not normally join in spoken conversation, or find this difficult for any reason, to join in dialogue with others. In the remainder of this chapter 'talk' will be used as a generic term, to include dialogue and other forms of talk above, so that talk 'is both the medium of learning and a tool for learning'. (Myhill et al., 2006, p7)

Central to facilitating effective talk is the language the teacher uses, particularly questioning. This is important because some studies claim that 70 per cent of talk in the classroom is the teacher. (Baumfield and Mroz, 2002) In a study of primary schools classes Myhill et al., (2006) found, in common with earlier studies (e.g. Hargreaves, Hislam and English, 2002), that 60 per cent of primary teacher's questions required a factual answer, that is questions which require a predetermined response. In addition, Tanner and Jones (2007, p323) report that in whole class teaching 'although teachers now ask more questions, most pupil responses remain very short, just five seconds on average, and involve three or fewer words'. This is perhaps not unexpected when much talk, especially in whole class teaching, is dominated by a 'recitation script' (Tharp and Gallimore, 1988) in which the IRF (Initiation, Response, Follow-on) model still dominates. Smith, Hardman and Higgins (2006, p444) report that this is

> *particularly prevalent in directive forms of teaching and often consists of closed teacher questions, brief pupil answers which teachers do not build upon, superficial praise*

rather than diagnostic feedback, and an emphasis on recalling information rather than genuine exploration of a topic. Recitation questioning therefore seeks predictable correct answers and only rarely are teachers' questions used to assist pupils to more complete or elaborated ideas.

The dominance of teacher questions also has an impact on the number of questions that pupils ask within the school setting. Evidence from earlier studies highlight how few questions pupils ask when they enter school compared to the many they ask their parents before entering school – from 50 per cent before school to 5 per cent upon entering nursery in one study. (Wells, 1986 and Tizard and Hughes, 1984 cited in Baumfield and Mroz, 2002)

Such a situation is hardly likely to encourage effective speaking and listening, so we need to consider how ICT, especially the IWB, can help to encourage use of higher order skills in talk and to encourage pupils to ask questions. There remains, however, a tension between the need for extended responses (and critical engagement with sources) and the requirements for 'pace' in lessons, but we will concentrate on the former as the latter is more straightforward to achieve.

Despite concerns about pace, ICT does provide a powerful tool for all aspects of talk. Using the full range of ICT (or ICTs if you prefer), you have a variety of options that can provide a stimulus to start dialogue, to facilitate extended dialogue using a variety of modes and media, and also a means of saving the 'dialogue' (in spoken and other modes discussed above) in a variety of formats which can be shared as necessary. As the person in control of access to ICT resources (at least in the first instance) the teacher is crucial, both in terms of facilitating dialogue through effective generic planning and classroom practice, but also in planning and facilitating the use of ICT for this purpose if it is the best option. We will now consider how ICT(s) can help to start, enable/extend, save and share 'talk'.

Stimulating or initiating 'talk'

Perhaps the most common use of ICT to initiate talk is as a whole class activity at the start of lessons. As a 'digital hub' (Cutrim Schmid, 2010), the IWB provides a range of options that can provoke classroom talk in this context. The use of the IWB should, however, always be considered alongside other non-ICT options, as sometimes they may provide something ICT cannot. It is very difficult for a video to compete with a student teacher (or other adult) rushing into the classroom dressed as an explorer wanting to tell the children about their adventures and asking the class to help save a colleague left behind – as witnessed in one Key Stage 1 lesson recently, along with background jungle noises playing over the class room speakers triggered through the IWB by the classroom assistant just before the teacher entered the room. (I should perhaps mention this student teacher was a drama specialist which helps!) What ICT *can* do is to then show the children high quality pictures of the jungle and videos of some of the animals that live there, as well as a map which allows you to zoom in from above down to ground level, not to mention opening and replying to an email from the explorer who was left behind (using a solar powered computer in case they ask!) – which you sent in a fit of creativity the night before whilst preparing your costume! Remember, all of this (except the dressing up) can be done in one place on the IWB, hence the digital hub. What is suggested here, as elsewhere, is that you use ICT for what it can do better than anything else. (If you can't face dressing up, then a video sent via email may be the next best thing – although more preparation is required and technical skill in recording, editing and sending/saving/accessing the video.) Although this activity starts as a whole class activity, the next step could be to discuss solutions with talk partners or small groups depending on the outcomes you wish to achieve.

Much recent research has focused on how the IWB can create a 'dialogic classroom' (Warwick et al., 2011) or encourage 'dialogic space' (Mercer et al., 2010). In both of these approaches, the IWB allows children to undertake collaborative learning with dialogue at the centre of the activity. This dialogue, and the use of the IWB, is set within a classroom pedagogy which allows for the development of the necessary talk skills and interactive skills to ensure children can work together effectively. In other words, we cannot assume that children will use talk or co-operate effectively without explicit teaching of relevant skills – see for example 'Talk Lessons' (Wegerif and Dawes, 2004) or Alexander's *Talk for Learning: teaching and learning through dialogue*. The role of interactive technologies (such as the IWB) would be in helping to initiate, define, undertake and record tasks. (Mercer et al., 2010) Table 6.1 (**http://dialogueiwb.educ.cam.ac.uk/resources/**) provides a useful framework for you as a teacher to both develop and observe how a class may interact and the associated behaviours to make it effective:

Tool to enable or extend 'talk'

It is important to reiterate here that ICT on its own will not facilitate an environment where talk will flourish. The talk needs to be situated in a wider pedagogic practice where pupils are partners in their learning. They also need opportunities to contribute ideas which both you and other children take seriously, and to ask and answer questions to build shared understanding. This is true at all ages, from reception through the end of the primary phase – and hopefully beyond. Central to this dialogic pedagogy (Alexander, 2008) is the posing of open-ended higher-order questions, contributing ideas, reflecting on what has been said and interpreting as necessary to help develop ideas. To aid in this process, Mercer et al., (2010, pp381–2) suggest that the IWB allows children easily to:

- access relevant material prepared by the teacher, which is relevant to the task, and move backward and forward through it according to their needs;
- annotate that material to take account of the developing discussions;
- remove and modify what they have written to take account of each others' views and their changing shared ideas;
- ensure that all members of the group can see what is being discussed, and what any member has contributed as annotations to the material;
- offer advice to each other about their annotations or other treatment of the material (e.g. the selection of specific slides or searches for relevant information).

Table 6.1 Using the IWB to support the development of dialogue in the classroom

In my classroom, we …	You will see us …	So that we can …
✓ respect, trust and listen to each other ✓ take risks and experiment by trying out new teaching approaches ✓ encourage children to be responsible for their own learning ✓ use good subject knowledge and awareness of our children's needs to help us use children's contributions to advance the dialogue taking place ✓ support children in a range of ways to enable them to share their views and ideas ✓ value talk in our lessons and plan for it to take place ✓ are willing to sometimes change our minds ✓ continue a dialogue over time, from lesson to lesson ✓ use a wide range of IWB features and resources to stimulate, enhance and record aspects of our learning	✓ sharing, discussing, commenting on and exploring our views and ideas ✓ asking each other questions ✓ showing that we consider other people's views ✓ sometimes trying to reach a shared understanding by building on what people say ✓ giving feedback and responding in a helpful way; being a 'critical friend' ✓ realising what we need or would like to learn and doing something about it! ✓ using what we already know to help us ✓ reasoning and thinking aloud ✓ telling each other what we have learnt when we have been thinking by ourselves ✓ using classroom resources, including the IWB, in different ways to help us in our learning ✓ saying why we agree or disagree with an idea	✓ realise what we still need or want to learn and how we might like to do it ✓ extend and refine what we already know ✓ explain our reasoning clearly ✓ help each other to understand things in a new way ✓ come to agreement ✓ express a range of views

While the above is true of the IWB, it may also be increasingly true that mobile devices (such as the ipad) can also offer the potential to do the same thing which can be useful in encouraging and extending talk in groups. In the above use of the IWB, we can see that ICT is allowing pupils to make their thinking explicit and open to all which is another important feature of enabling and extending talk. This is a central feature of using the IWB in this context and can only take place in a supportive classroom atmosphere, where mistakes are seen as acceptable and a step to further knowledge. It is suggested, that to be effective such an approach needs to be introduced at an early age and be part of a whole-school strategy. At the very least, it needs to be consistent when *you* are teaching a class. This is not always straightforward due to pressures of time but, if time is given in planning to providing opportunities for such discussion it is more likely to happen.

WHAT DO YOU THINK?

You are teaching a lesson using an IWB. You use the wrong feature and the work you have prepared disappears. You have reassured pupils it is all right to make mistakes in your class but what do you do next?

Saving/recording 'talk'

Once the talk is generated, which, as we have seen above, can take many forms using many modes and medias, it is also useful to be able to save or record it. Each different mode or media may require specific knowledge of how to save and share, depending on the hardware and software involved, but generic principles can be applied to all. Central to acquiring the necessary skills is the belief that talk has merit and is worth sharing. As in much written work, and in accordance with curriculum expectations, we need to consider the target audience for the talk both in terms of style and in taking account of their developmental capabilities – with young children who cannot read, it would be inappropriate to use text but video may be appropriate. The options for sharing are many and include:

- Email
- Website
- Intranet
- Pen drive
- Secure online storage: e.g. Dropbox or other similar – which can also be synchronised with home and school computers or other devices (e.g. ipads).

The whole process, not just the end result, of constructing, saving and sharing work should be part of the educational process and can reflect the belief that pupils are actively involved in their learning. With mobile devices the saving (and sharing) does not even have to be done by you, as many mobile devices allow easy uploading facilities which can be operated by very young children. In this case, the role of the teacher is really to lead the process (for instance a discussion about options and ensure the right questions are asked – e.g. about online security) rather than complete the steps in the process – although you need to be familiar with the process to help if required. In saving work on networks, or online storage facilities, you are also creating digital portfolios. In this case the audience is two-fold: the first is the pupils themselves, to aid in reflecting on their work; the second, others in school and beyond – including their parents.

As work is stored, and added to over time, there is evidence that compiling and then using digital portfolios (that is the electronic storage of work) in the primary schools is an effective stimulus for talk (Wall et al., 2006), as well as an enjoyable and valuable activity which encourages pupils to think not only about their work, but also about themselves as learners. (McLeod and Vasinda, 2009).

Sharing 'talk'

As 'talk' becomes available in real time and online, we need to consider potential audiences beyond those immediately involved. Beyond the confines of the classroom, Dawes, Mercer and Wegerif (2000) remind us that the 'C' in ICT refers to communication, both sharing information and jointly constructing knowledge. They suggest further that, with advances in ICT, this should be communication within the classroom and at a distance. As such we can consider how ICT can contribute to sharing talk between:

- individuals
- groups
- whole class
- classrooms within a school
- schools

Podcasts

One way of sharing talk is to use podcasts. In simple terms, a podcast is an audio recording which is hosted on a website, such as your school website, and can be listened to anywhere in the world with an Internet connection. Deal (2007, p2) suggest podcasts are normally linked thematically and 'are accompanied by a file called a "feed" that allows listeners to subscribe to the series and receive new episodes automatically'. In creating the finished sound file, it is unlikely that a complete file can be recorded in one 'take', so it is likely that the sound editing program will be needed. There are many options available commercially, and also programs such as Audacity (**http://audacity.sourceforge.net/**) are available freely and allow you to edit and save sound in a variety of formats. Using this type of program, or other free programs such as Garage Band on Apple computers, it is possible to add musical introductions and other features. In addition to these slightly more complicated programs, it is also possible to create and upload podcasts on a mobile devices such as iphones, or android-based phones, using programs such as Audioboo (**http://audioboo.fm**) – although these do not allow the creation of different tracks, so everything has to be done in real time as a live event. It may be, however, that this less sophisticated types of software could allow you to create and upload podcasts in a variety of settings outside the classroom, such as on a school trip. This can also be useful in relating to work across the curriculum (see Chapter 8), as programs such as Audioboo are also linked to mapping services which show the location of the Podcast was recorded. The caveat to using anywhere except for your school website to host your podcasts, is that ultimately you have less control and you need to read the host sites terms and conditions carefully.

To create a podcast, the basic requirements are a microphone (built into many computers and mobile devices), a computer and an internet connection. Beyond these basics, however, we need to understand the purpose of a podcast before proceeding. In the context of this chapter, the purpose is to share 'talk', but this talk should have a purpose. To be effective, a podcast should be more than the recording of the lesson or recording of an event (such as a class assembly) which takes place in real time – although there is no reason that extracts from such recordings should be included in a podcast. Such events as 'of the moment' and there may be better ways (such as video) of recording these, and the recording would have a different purpose. This distinction is important because, as Middleton (2009, p144) points out, when discussing the use of podcasts in higher education, 'disappointingly, the term is synonymous in some quarters with the transmission of the teacher's knowledge through the distribution of recorded lectures'. We have seen throughout this book that although ICT is good at transmitting knowledge, we need to use it more imaginatively. In this case, we need to see how podcasts can be used with primary pupils to help them work collaboratively to co-construct knowledge and understanding. To do this, they need to be actively involved both in the design and construction of podcasts.

CASE STUDY

Examples of primary school pod casts are increasingly common. One example is The Downs CE primary school, whose web site (**http://tinyurl.com/3ot9dod**) gives detailed notes on how the pupils produce their podcasts. In summary,

> We begin each week by deciding what we're going to put into each show, and organising who is going to make the different parts of it. Some of us might find and record jokes, others might research and record a news article, whilst another group might prepare and record an interview with a member of staff, or with a special guest. ... It's really difficult trying to make The Downs FM in our usual lesson time because there are so many children in the class, and it's not very easy giving them all a job to do. So, we usually prepare for our shows during our lunchtimes. Sometimes we record the show in front of our class, as this gives us an audience (who can also get involved in the show), but that makes things a little more nerve-wracking!

In this case, uploading of the finished file and setting up the relevant feed to allow subscribers to receive the broadcast, is done by the class teacher. Many schools, however, will have an ICT co-ordinator who could do this, but the process is not complicated, and can be done from within a variety of programs. Before starting to produce your own podcasts it would be best to listen to the work of other primary schools, such as the one above. Podcasts can often be found on school websites, or withinanother forums, such as blogs.

Although it may seem from the above that the process of creating podcasts is complicated, some advantages, in common with all material posted on a VLE or website, are that they:

- are produced specifically for the pupils in the class for school;
- are available 'on demand' at any time of the day and from anywhere with an Internet connection;
- have the potential to help pupils with special needs;
- are useful if pupils miss lessons;
- can help with communication with parents who can listen to podcasts with their children;
- can be helpful for pupils with English as an Additional Language (EAL);
- can motivate pupils if they are involved in the production of materials;

- can help develop teamwork if groups of children are involved in production;
- can help to develop literacy skills (such as writing scripts or interview questions, or writing for a particular audience) and also allows pupils to develop and practise their speaking and listening skills;
- add another 'layer' to the text as it can be easier to recognise, or add, emotion in the spoken word – it also personalises the experience for the children to hear other children of their own age;
- are portable as they can be downloaded onto any MP3 player, computer, ipod, or even burned onto CDs – all of these mean that Podcasts can be listened to anywhere from the pupils bedroom to a car on a journey.

To balance this list of advantages, we also need to consider the disadvantages of podcasting compared to other forms of communication. These include:

- It is difficult to include links to websites in podcasts compared to text-based material where these can be included as clickable links;
- It may take a longer time to refine the finished product compared to a piece of writing, as they are more difficult to edit;
- There is a degree of technical knowledge required;
- As above, it may be difficult to involve the whole class actively in producing the podcasts.

As well as creating your own podcasts, there are also others available that can be used in lessons. These can normally be listened to directly from the website by clicking on the relevant file name – although the IWB, or computer, will have to have speakers attached and the sound turned up. An added bonus of podcasts, which does not relate directly to your pupils, is that they can also be used as part of staff training and CPD work, with the same advantages as above.

Reading

We have already seen above that the reading of text alone (one mode of communication) is not sufficient on its own. An added complication is that, as a 'situated social practice' (Moss, 2008, p73), reading can have different interpretations, motivations and expectations, on the part of both teachers and pupils. In addition, these may be at variance with social practice in another setting, such as at home. In the context of the school, reading often has a highly prescribed interpretation and purpose as defined in a curriculum. For example, the current National Curriculum for England at Key Stage 1 for reading includes requirement to teach 'Word recognition and graphic knowledge' ('They should be taught phonemic awareness and phonic knowledge to decode and encode words'), 'Understanding text', 'Reading for information', 'Literature' and 'Language structure and variation' using a range of fiction and non-fiction texts.

In a curriculum, success in reading can be limited to, for example, the successful reading aloud (or just 'decoding' – see above) of words from the text (script) without any deviation, the successful retrieval of specified information from a (non-fiction) book or answering questions about the text which shows an agreement with the views of the examiner/teacher. (Moss, 2008) Such an interpretation may, however, may be at odds with the other more idiosyncratic views of the nature and purpose of reading on the part of the pupil. In addition, the emphasis on text-based resources may not reflect their experience of reading other multimodal sources, such as games or web pages.

We have already considered the use of computer games in Chapter 1, but there is some evidence that 'appropriately designed computer games can play a useful role in helping some struggling readers at home' (Holmes, 2011, p15). As we have seen earlier, however, although Commercial Off-The Shelf Software (COTS) provides authentic gaming experiences that children will be familiar with from home, it does not mean that the reading skills required, or developed, will be helpful in the school context. Again, we see the tension between the demands of the school curriculum and the real life experience of many children.

WHAT DO YOU THINK?

Should equipping pupils with the reading ability to meet the prescribed needs of a national curriculum be more important than preparing them to read material of their own choosing in a range of formats? *While it could be argued that meeting the curriculum requirements would enable pupils to meet these needs, in an ever-changing world of technology, is using traditional paper-based texts a suitable first choice of approach? Should digital books or reading from a screen in a games-style format or from a mobile device be the first choice of medium? When will technology replace books – or will it?*

Despite this, some ICT resources are helpful in developing reading but, as with 'real' books, the resources need to be used with care as on their own they are not enough. For example, E-books may be useful in the classroom, particularly with an IWB for whole class work, but there is evidence that adult support is vital for progress to be made with young children in phonological awareness and emergent word writing. (Korat et al., 2011) This is in line with other research that suggests that when using ICT the role of the teacher as guide is just as important as it is in other teaching situations without ICT (Postholm, 2006).

Beyond specific ICT reading resources (such as talking books), there is also a role for ICT in the recording of more conventional reading practice, such as reading to an adult. We have already seen that such work can be recorded and used for evidence or record of achievement files, or as part of a digital portfolio – see above.

Writing

There are many pragmatic uses of ICT in the teaching of writing, such as direct teaching of phonics using the IWB, followed by reinforcement using computer programs. This is using the features of ICT effectively, but is by necessity largely teacher-centred (teacher at IWB) or teacher-directed (teacher chooses programs to be used and when to use them). In order to make effective use of ICT we need to consider how we can also be become pupil-centred. One of the key features of ICT which helps in this, is that pupils can use the provisionality feature (see Chapter 1) to experiment and interact with text (Davies and O'Sullivan, 2002). This can only take place, however, within the confines of the curriculum – unless ICT is used more creatively in extra-curricular activities such as clubs. As with reading above, there remains a possible tension about the nature and purpose of writing between what the curriculum demands and the views of the pupils themselves. The 'official' view of the current National Curriculum for England at Key Stage 1 is that pupils should be taught the following:

- Composition
- Planning and drafting
- Punctuation
- Spelling (Spelling strategies, Checking spelling)
- Handwriting and presentation
- Standard English
- Language structure

It remains open to debate how many of these requirements would be relevant to pupils in their own life in a world of 'text-speak' and informal grammar. For the purposes of this book, however, we can limit ourselves to considering how ICT can impact on writing in the primary school setting. As we have discussed above, pupils have many modes of writing available to them in schools, as well as a potential world-wide audience for their writing and we will explore some below.

Perhaps the most obvious use, and earliest, of ICT in writing is as what Papert (1993) called a 'writing instrument'. It is a sign of the speed of advances in this area that, even in the second edition of his seminal work, Papert still retained the paragraph which claimed that 'most newspapers now provide their staff with "word processing" computer systems. Many writers who work at home are acquiring their own computers, and the computer terminal is steadily displacing the typewriter as the secretary's basic tool'. (Papert, 1993, p30) The ubiquitous nature of PCs in homes, offices and schools today, and the power and sophistication of the 'word processing' packages, signal the speed of progress – let alone being able to word process with voice recognition, touch screen technology the use of hyperlinks and moving graphics!

When using ICT in writing, Wegerif and Dawes (2004, p106) suggest that 'for children in primary schools, developing the capacity to interact effectively with computers requires the teaching of a classic literacy and ICT literacy'. They further suggest that 'classic literacy, ICT literacy and oracy are interlinked. Ways of writing begin as ways of talking'. (p107) As we have seen above that ICT, especially the IWB, has the potential to be very effective at encouraging talk, we can see that such activities are also contributing to the development of writing. These activities could not take place without specific ICT skills (ICT literacy) on the part of the teacher and the pupil, and planning when to teach these in advance of when they are required is, as we saw earlier, central to effective lessons. If such planning takes place, however,

> *Digital technologies have opened up new opportunities to children to learn about how texts are constructed. Whereas in the past, producing printed texts, animations and films required specialist technology and skills, new digital technologies have made it possible*

for people to produce all kinds of texts from their own homes. Using new technologies it should be possible to encourage children to acquire their own experience of being producers of texts, becoming involved in choosing how to assemble resources to generate meanings. (Eagle, 2008, p12)

An important challenge for primary teachers is ensuring that all these possibilities are exploited, but there are obvious implications for their own knowledge of ICT. If these opportunities are exploited, and once writing begins, another feature of ICT comes into play which is the ability to communicate with others quickly.

Collaborative writing

Collaborative writing, within and between classes and schools, is possible with many online websites (such as Primary Pad – **http://primarypad.com/** or Meeting Words – **http://meetingwords.com/** or Google Docs), although these are not always free and you need to ensure any projects you create are open to members only. It is also important to check that your projects are not going to be deleted after a certain period of time, particularly if they provide evidence for assessment or records of work. (The ability to have these features may be one of the differences between free and subscriptions services.) Despite these caveats, the ability to collaborate in real time, with each pupil's text being highlighted in a different colour, can provide a real stimulus for writing activities.

Another platform for collaborative writing is a wiki. Wikis are

websites that allow their users to create and edit content. Different wiki services offer different levels of functionality, although they all include functionality for editing by more than one person, either restricted to members or open to a wider public. They commonly also include the ability to compare previous versions of a page, a separate page for discussion and a user history that tracks the time and content of contributions and edits. (Grant, 2006, p105)

There is currently little research evidence examining how wikis are used with primary children in the UK, but some evidence of primary pupils in Hong Kong suggests that wikis help to develop teamwork, encourage peer-to-peer interaction and facilitate online group work. If teachers also join in and post feedback, this helps in the process of constructing group writing. (Woo et al., 2011) Some caveats for the use of wikis will be familiar from earlier chapters and suggest the need for adequate training for both pupils and staff, as well as factors such as class size and instructional design (Engstrom and Jewett, 2005). In particular, the wiki model is difficult with whole class use at the same time as a page cannot be edited by more than one person at a time, although this would not apply if groups or individuals were working on different pages one at a time. Similar possibilities may exist for the use of blogs with primary pupils, but again there is currently a paucity of research literature in this area.

Creative writing

One of the most significant changes brought about with advances in ICT is the potential for primary pupils to write for a large range of new and different audiences and purposes. Bennett (2004:47) suggests these could include:

- Communicating with real and fictional people via fax, email, webchat, and so on
- Reading and contributing to online stories
- Creating web pages to communicate information and ideas

The fictional characters in the first bullet could include those from traditional written texts, or from Talking Books or even from ICT-based games. The latter has also been used as a stimulus for creative writing in terms of what happened next?, composing new scenarios/challenges and new endings or writing character sketches for individuals within the games – see for instance Sandford et al., (2006).

Another important feature of ICT is that it can produce high quality presentation of work in a variety of formats, regardless of the ability of the pupils concerned. This is not to suggest that presentation is more important than content, but it can encourage pupils to take pride in their work and may also help those who may be discouraged if their handwriting is not a strong point. In addition, modern word processors can help pupils of all ages to be creative in how the writing is presented (think 'Charlie and Lola'!), or to achieve effects of characterisations (e.g. a different font for each character to reflect their speech) or, for instance, to make a text (or part of it, such as a treasure map found in the story) appear old to reflect its setting.

ACTIVITY

On your own or in a group, make a list of positive and negative points of using ICT devices to present written work for two contrasting age groups within the primary school. If working with others, discuss why you have made these decisions. If working on your own or with others, see if there are common features to each age group or if there are different and distinct reasons for your choices.

Another way of using ICT in creative writing is demonstrated by resources such as Teachers TV (now archived under different websites, such as the TES, due to funding cuts), which provide a series of 'short but dramatic' video clips to serve as 'Story Starts'. These are aimed at children from year one to year six, and can be played on the IWB and class room speakers to provide a very effective stimulus to creative writing. For example, one set of story starts provide seven different clips, including 'an alluring jewellery shop, a ghostly graveyard and a tunnel with a warning'. (**http://tinyurl.com/3n2edry**). The main activity can remain traditional story writing with pen and paper, but ICT is used for something that it is good at and cannot be done easily another way. A follow-up activity for this could be for children themselves to use ICT to create their own story starts, both for other classes in the school and for the same year group next year. Other examples include clips aimed specifically at Year one and Year 2, which use a variety of puppetry techniques to begin the story of traditional tales such as Red Riding Hood, The Miserly Farmer, The Key in the Sea, The Raja's Secret and Aladdin (**http://tinyurl.com/3ma7rom**).

The IWB can also be used effectively to both collect vocabulary and to plot storylines (by dragging and dropping ideas) as a whole class or group. Remember that the IWB is not just for the teacher, but can be used as a tool for pupils in group work whilst others work on other resources or activities. In addition, by connecting a wireless keyboard to the computer attached to the IWB, it is easy to pass this around to achieve group or class word banks, stories or poetry. In this activity, pupils are again working collaboratively (they can choose who has the keyboard next) and need to take account of the work of others that has preceded theirs. You can also easily step in (by reclaiming the keyboard) to add your own contributions to extend or refocus the activity without having to stop the flow of the lesson and give verbal instructions.

As we have seen above, the IWB in particular offers many affordances for literacy activities. However, effective planning is the key to making best use of the technology and making full use of its features. To help with this planning, Table 6.2 below (adapted from Kennewell and Beauchamp, 2007) provides some examples of how the IWB can provide both potential for, and structure in, literacy activities – but as we will see later the examples in the table can be adapted for other areas of the curriculum or indeed cross-curricular activities.

Table 6.2 Possible actions for which ICT provides potential and structure

Action	Meaning	Example
Composing	Ideas can be recorded accurately as they arise	Students record vocabulary for class poem – exemplar for individual work.
Editing	The data stored and displayed can be changed easily with no trace of the original	Individual students revising their poems on laptop after group or whole-class discussion using IWB
Selecting	Choice of pre-existing resource or procedure can be made (e.g. from a list)	Students select the appropriate words from a list of vocabulary in a language exercise – drag and drop on IWB
Comparing	Features of same object from different views or different items displayed can be compared	Teacher displays pictures of flower taken from different angles or different flowers looking for common features and discussing vocabulary for writing in science
Retrieving	Stored resources can easily be retrieved for use	Teacher retrieves examples of same work (e.g. creative writing or pupil's presentation) from different classes or students retrieve files to complete work or demonstrate to peers
Apprehending	The display (text, images, sound, diagrams) makes it easier for students to see or interpret	An image or sound effect can be added to illustrate the meaning of an unfamiliar word on the IWB or using IWB to read a 'big book' or talking book
Focusing	Attention can be drawn to particular aspects of a process or representation	Teacher uses the 'reveal' tool to focus attention or uses zoom/magnify to look closer at a seed to identify how it becomes attached to an animal for dispersal in preparation – new vocabulary

(continued)

Table 6.2 *continued.*

Action	Meaning	Example
Transforming	The way that the data are displayed can be changed	Students and/or teacher discuss the effect of changing font on the appearance of a newspaper article they have written about the school fayre
Role playing	Activities can be carried out in a way which is similar to activity in the 'real world'	Students use the IWB to write a menu for a café in the 'play corner'
Collating	The facility to bring together a variety of items from different sources into a single resource	Students collect ideas (e.g. pictures, words or artefacts) using digital cameras and laptops (or ipods) from around the school grounds review on visualiser and IWB for class project work
Sharing	The facility to communicate and interchange resources and ideas easily with others	Teacher retrieves PowerPoint presentation on grammar compiled by colleagues from school network
Annotating	Notes can be added to a process or representation at the time of use	Teacher annotates the PowerPoint presentation or students annotate a picture for work in history
Repeating	An automated or stored process can be repeated at will	Students can replay an animation of the flow of blood through a heart when writing discussing or writing an explanation.
Modelling	A process can be simulated by representing relationships between variables	Students enter different food quantities into spreadsheet and watch effect on graphs representing high-energy foods, food for growth – discussion and cumulative talk
Cumulating	Building up a representation of knowledge in a progressive manner	Students compile a group presentation (using a variety of media) over the course of a term/topic before presenting to peers
Revisiting	Repeating an activity or returning with a different focus	A list of ideas generated by the class at the start of the lesson is reviewed following an Internetsearch and discussion
Undoing	Reversing an action	A tentative idea or solution to a problem is removed without trace
Questioning	Piece of dialogue requiring a response	'What other adjectives could we use there'?
Prompting	Action or piece of dialogue which suggests what someone should do	'Try to find another word which means the same thing there'
Responding	Action which is contingent on a previous question/prompt	Change 'big' to 'enormous' in example of text on IWB when prompted

The examples above could easily be added to and we could go on considering ways that ICT is beneficial in literacy, but in reality it is suggested that the potential is only limited by the pedagogic vision of the teacher. One of the problems with this, however, is that for every new approach, teachers have to consider how they can be assessed effectively.

SUMMARY

In this chapter we have explored how new literacies are needed in all areas of English to help make sense of, and explore, an increasing range of modes of communication. ICT enables a wide range of 'talk' to take place and be shared, both within the school and beyond. As part of this sharing, we have seen how ICT can encourage collaboration, for instance in writing in a range of forms. This does not, however, mean that traditional talk is neglected. It is suggested that pupil talk can in fact be enhanced and enriched,as ICT provides a powerful set of tools for developing all aspects of talk. Using the full range of ICT you have a variety of options that can provide a stimulus to start dialogue, to facilitate extended dialogue using a variety of modes and media, and also a means of saving the 'dialogue' (in spoken and other modes discussed above) in a variety of formats which can be shared as necessary. We have also seen how some ICT resources can helpful in reading but, as with 'real' books, the resources need to be used with care, as on their own they are not enough. In fact, this same caveat applies to all use of ICT in English, and indeed other subjects. Your skills as a teacher remain vital in ensuring that ICT is only used when it enhances learning and teaching, and not just because it is there.

References

Baumfield,V. and Mroz, M. (2002), 'Investigating pupils' questions in the primary classroom', *Educational Research*, 44:2, 129–140.

Bennett, R., Hamill, A. and Pickford, T. (2007), *Progression in Primary ICT*, Oxford: David Fulton

Bennett, R. (2004), *Using ICT in Primary English Teaching*, Exeter: Learning Matters.

Cheung, C. K. (2005): 'The relevance of media education in primary schools in Hong Kong in the age of new media: a case study', *Educational Studies*, 31:4, 361–74.

Cutrim Schmid, E. (2010) 'Using the Interactive Whiteboardas a "Digital Hub"', PraxisFremdsprachenunterricht,04/10. pp12–15.

Davies, H. and O'Sullivan, O. (2002), 'Literacy and ICT in the primary classroom: the role of the Teacher', in Loveless, A. and Dore, B. (eds) (2002) *ICT in the Primary School*, Buckingham: Open University Press.

Dawes, L., Mercer, N. and Wegerif, R. (2000), 'Extending Talking and Reasoning Skills Using ICT' in Leask, M. and Meadows, J. (eds) (2000), *Teaching and Learning with ICT in the Primary School*, London: Routledge.

Deal, A. (2007) *Podcasting – a teaching with technology white paper*, Pittsburgh, PA: Carnegie Mellon University.

Eagles, S. (2006), 'How might research on family reading practices inform the design of interactive digital resources for pre-school children?' in Eagle et al., (2006), pp3–17.

Eagle, S., Manches, A., O'Malley, C., Plowman, L. and Sutherland, R. (2008), *From research to design: Perspectives on early years and digital technologies*, Bristol:Futurelab.

Engstrom, M. E., and Jewett, D. (2005), Collaborative learning the Wiki way. *TechTrends*, 49(6), 12.

Grant, L. (2009), 'I DON'T CARE DO UR OWN PAGE!' A case study of using wikis for collaborative work in a UK secondary school, *Learning, Media and Technology*, 34:2, 105–17.

Hargreaves, L., Hislam, J. and English, E. (2002), 'Pedagogical dilemmas in the National Literacy Strategy: primary teachers' perceptions, reflections and classroom behaviour', *Cambridge Journal of Education*, 32(1), 9–26.

Higgins, S. and Muijs, D. (1999), 'ICT and numeracy in primary schools', in Thompson, I. (ed.), *Issues in Teaching Numeracy in Primary Schools*, Buckingham: Open University Press, 103–16.

Holmes, W. (2011), 'Using game-based learning to support struggling readers at home', *Learning, Media and Technology*, 36: 1, 5–19.

John, P.D. and Wheeler, S. (2008), *The Digital Classroom: Harnessing technology for the future of learning and teaching*, London: Routledge.

Kennewell, S. and Beauchamp, G. (2007), 'The features of interactive whiteboards and their influence on learning', *Learning, Media and Technology*, 32:3, 227–41.

Korat, O., Shamir, A. and Arbiv, L. (2011), 'E-books as support for emergent writing with and without adult assistance', *Education and Information Technologies*, 16, 301–18.

Kress, G. and Jewitt, C. (2008), 'Introduction', in Kress, G. and Jewitt, C. (eds) (2008), *Multimodal Literacy*, New York: Peter Lang Publishing. 1–18.

Matthewman, S. (2009), 'Discerning literacy', in Sutherland, R., Robertson, S. and John, P., *Improving Classroom Learning with ICT*, London: Routledge, 115–37.

McLeod, J.K. and Vasinda, S. (2009), 'Electronic portfolios: perspectives of students, teachers and parents', *Education and Information Technologies*, 14:29–38.

Mercer, N., Kershner, R., Warwick, P., and Kleine Staarman, J. (2010), 'Can the interactive whiteboard help to provide "dialogic space" for children's collaborative activity?' *Language and Education*, 24(5), 367–84.

Middleton, A. (2009) 'Beyond podcasting: creative approaches to designing educational audio', *ALT-J*, 17: 2, 143–55.

Moss, G. (2008), 'Putting the text back into practice: junior-age non-fiction as objects of design', in Kress, G. and Jewitt, C. (eds) (2008) *Multimodal Literacy*, New York: Peter Lang Publishing, 73–87.

Myhill, D., Jones, S. and Hopper, R. (2006), *Talking, Listening, Learning*, Maidenhead: Open University Press.

Owen, M., Grant, L., Sayers, S. and Facer, K. (2006), *Social software and learning*, Bristol: Futurelab.

Postholm, M.B. (2006), 'The teacher's role when pupils work on task using ICT in project work', *Educational Research*, 48: 2, 155–75.

Rudd, A. and Tyldesley, A. (2006), *Literacy and ICT in the Primary School: A Creative Approach to English*, London: David Fulton.

Sandford, R., Ulicsak, M., Facer, K. and Rudd, T. (2006), *Teaching with Games: Using commercial off-the-shelf computer games in formal education*, Bristol: Futurelab.

Smith, F., Hardman, F. and Higgins, S. (2006), 'The impact of interactive whiteboards on teacher– student interaction in the National Literacy and Numeracy Strategies', *British EducationalResearch Journal*, 32(3), 443–57.

Turner, S. and McCullouch, J. (2004), *Making Connections in Primary Mathematics: A Practical Guide*, London: David Fulton.

Wall, K. , Higgins, S. , Miller, J. and Packard, N. (2006), 'Developing digital portfolios: investigating how digital portfolios can facilitate pupil talk about learning', *Technology, Pedagogy and Education*, 15: 3,261–273.

Warwick, P., Hennessy, S. and Mercer, N. (2011), 'Promoting teacher and school development through co-enquiry: developing interactive whiteboard use in a "dialogic classroom"', *Teachers and Teaching*, 17: 3. 303–24.

Way, J. and Beardon, T. (eds) (2003), *ICT and Primary Maths*, Maidenhead: Open University Press.

Wegerif, R. and Dawes, L. (2004), *Thinking and learning with ICT: raising achievement in primary classrooms*, London: Routledge.

Woo, M., Chu, S., Ho, A., and Li, X. (2011), 'Using a Wiki to scaffold primary-school students' collaborative writing', *Educational Technology & Society,* 14 (1), 43–54.

Useful websites

Using the IWB to Support Classroom Dialogue: **http://dialogueiwb.educ.cam.ac.uk/** Project based at the University of Cambridge (UK) that includes a range of professional development resources, videos and further reading.

CHAPTER 7

ICT and Mathematics in Key Stages 1 and 2

In this chapter we will consider the important role that talk also plays in teaching mathematics. We will explore how the use of signs and symbols in mathematical language makes this process potentially challenging and can lead to misconceptions. We will examine how ICT can help to address these misconceptions, as well as how it can be used in the areas of Number, Shape, Space and Measure and Handling Data.

ICT and mathematics in key stages 1 and 2

In mathematics in the primary school, language is central to effective teaching and learning. It is particularly important that you and your pupils have a shared understanding of the language you use in mathematics and how this may vary from use of the same words or phrases in other contexts – both in the curriculum and outside of school. An additional complication is that, as well as words, the mathematical language 'uses symbols to represent numbers and number operations (such as the word "nine" to represent this quantity or the written sign "+" to represent combining quantities)'. (Manches, 2006, p18) Turner and McCullough (2004, pp2–3) suggest that resultant ambiguity can be identified in the following ways:

1. Meaning that differs according to whether the word is used as a noun or a verb. For example: the word note can mean an instruction [verb], a form of currency [noun] and a musical symbol [noun].
2. Words that are derived from the same root, but that have a different meaning in an everyday context, e.g. the net of a shape and a fishing net. Some words in this category have two or more mathematical meanings that are used in a mathematical context (e.g. left denotes direction and also identifies a numerical remainder).
3. Homophones and homonyms, e.g. one/won; count/Count Ferdinand.

If pupils do not understand that language is being used in a mathematical context, it is possible that they will develop misconceptions (see below) through misunderstanding the context in which the word is used (hence perhaps adopting an inappropriate strategy), or not understanding what they are required to do. It is important to note that this applies to both spoken language and to words that appear in other forms, such as work you have prepared on the IWB, a worksheet or a text book. Perhaps the key idea here is that, if necessary, you need to identify potential confusing language at the planning stage, plan how to address this / introduce it, and continue to make it explicit throughout the lesson that you are using words in a mathematical context. This should be continued in subsequent lessons in mathematics and reinforced in other areas of the curriculum – questions could include: 'what did this word mean when we used it in maths? What else can it mean? What does in mean in our science/ music/etc lesson today'? – to ensure pupils fully understand words before using and applying them. (A useful summary of vocabulary and possible misunderstandings in mathematics can be found in Turner and McCullough, 2004, pp7–10.)

TIP

Although we have discussed the use of language in mathematics, the same concerns and processes apply in any area of the curriculum (most) that uses specialist language which has more than one meaning, such as music, science and geography.

Having decided on appropriate mathematical language for your class (both written and spoken), and made clear any misunderstandings about its use, we can now consider some key areas of mathematics teaching in the primary school where ICT can help.

Misconceptions

The first of these is in addressing misconceptions. Hollins and Whitby (2001, p2) provide a useful summary of how this applies to science, which has resonance in other areas of the curriculum, when they state:

> *concepts will always be rooted in our own previous experience, which will influence our attempts at understanding. There is a sense in which our concepts can never be 'wrong', as they are a reflection of our level of understanding at that time. They may not, however, concur with accepted scientific ideas and may therefore be 'misconceptions'. For us to be able to alter our conceptual understanding, new experiences must be encountered which challenge the existing concept. If this challenge involves too big a leap from currently held ideas, the new ideas will be dismissed out of hand, or lip-service will be paid to them while the original concept remains intact. If the challenge involves a sufficiently different rethink of the currently held concept, then the concept may be adapted or changed to fit the new experience; learning will therefore take place. A major part of our role as teachers must therefore be to ascertain children's current understanding and then structure new experiences to bring about this learning.*

The ability of ICT to present ideas in a variety of ways can help to structure new experiences, but only if you as the teacher have sufficient understanding on the area yourself. If this is not the case, you are in danger of perpetuating the misconceptions of pupils or introducing new ones of your own! As Murphy (2006, p229) states 'teachers' knowledge of mathematics should be of sufficient depth to enable them to represent it in a variety of ways and to be flexible enough to enable them to interpret students' ideas and address misconceptions'.

It is, however, important to state clearly that misconceptions are not always a bad thing. In fact quite the opposite may be true at times. In mathematics, misconceptions can 'often reveal much about children's thinking and how they acquire – or not, is the case may be – an understanding of complex mathematical concepts'. (Cockburn and Littler, 2008, p3) Exploring how children acquire their ideas is perhaps the most fundamental part of finding suitable teaching methods to address a misconception – and to inform your future teaching to ensure that you do either introduce new misconceptions or reinforce others. In addition, discussing ideas with pupils can also allow you to make the important distinction between an error and a misconception. Dawes (2005, p14) states that errors in mathematics (but this is equally applicable in other areas) can be made for many reasons including 'carelessness; misinterpretation of symbols or text; lack of relevant experience or knowledge related to that mathematical topic/learning objective/concept; a lack of awareness or inability to check the answer given; or the result of a misconception'. In addition, don't forget to consider the more obvious explanations such as you made the task too hard!

TIP

Have you checked that other adults in the classroom are aware of possible misconceptions before the lesson starts?

Unless we know how the problem is formed, it is very difficult to 'transform' (see Schulman in Chapter 2) your own understanding of a topic into something that children may understand. It could also be argued that by guiding children back through the same process by which they acquired the knowledge in the first place, but 'correcting' where it went wrong (by new experiences, explanation and so on), may be the most effective way of arriving at an alternative conception. (This does make the assumption that it was not you who causes the misconception in the first place; in which case you know how it was formed!) This can only be done if you know how pupil's views were formed. So, how can ICT help in establishing this?

In earlier chapters, we have seen that ICT can allow pupils to record their thoughts in a wide variety of ways. They are able to write, draw, record both sound and video, or any combination of these depending on their age and ability. All of these activities can be done as an individual or as a group and of course saved to be shared with the others in the classroom or elsewhere. In the latter instance, asking your pupils to explain their understanding of something to another group of pupils in another school can be a very good pretext for an assessment activity – but is hopefully equally valid as a teaching activity for the pupils in the other school. It is very important in this instance, to realise the transformative and empowering nature of ICT in enabling someone who may, for instance, find writing difficult but can happily make a voice recording of their thoughts. This may be especially true of children with particular needs which make expressing their thoughts difficult in more conventional ways. Central to this discussion is the realisation that voice recordings or digital images have equal worth to some more traditional more traditional methods of assessment.

Examples of misconceptions

Let us consider how ICT help address a misconception in both key stage 1 and 2, in this instance in mathematics. Before doing so, however, we should be clear about the distinction in mathematics between 'procedural' and 'conceptual' knowledge, that is,knowing how and when to use computations. (Nunes, 2001) In the examples that follow, we are concerned with conceptual knowledge, but ICT can also help with procedural knowledge – but in a more straightforward way such as using the IWB for explicit teaching, modelling and practice of relevant procedures.

Key stage 1: A new animal house for the zoo

In a reception class the pupils are learning mathematical language relating to size. The scenario is that they have been asked (by email) to design a new house for some of the animals in the local zoo. It becomes obvious that many children think giraffes are very small and smaller than hippos. After discussion it emerges that the toy hippo and giraffe the children play with in the classroom are the source of the misconception. Obviously it would be ideal to let the children see the real animals but, as this may not be possible, movies of the real animals are a useful substitute – you decide not to use cartoons as they may reinforce the same or different misconceptions (such as that animals can talk!). You find a suitable video on a zoo website and show the whole class on the IWB – you have made sure that the video contains suitable reference points (like a human adult) the pupils may be familiar with (in the absence of real animals or life-size models!) to help them realise the relative size. During and after the video the children are able to use suitable language like, 'they are taller than a teacher' which would help them design the new homes. The same exercise is then repeated with a hippo. After this is completed, you must then ensure that the relative size to each other is discussed. Do not assume that just because they can make correct relative size statements about each animal compared to humans, that they will automatically make the relative judgement between the animals. Remember that the objective was to realise that giraffes are taller than hippos and hence would need different houses; the humans are just a familiar comparator to aid this concept – in the absence of a trip to the zoo!

ACTIVITY

Discuss with others if children were stating that the giraffe is 'bigger than an adult', would you accept it? If not, why not?

You may find the example of good practice from Ofsted of interest in this context:

Prime practice: language development	Learning mathematical language in a Reception class. The children's language and conceptual understanding were developed securely through a range of well planned activities that provided plenty of opportunity for them to use new words, make comparisons and reason.

The teacher was working outside with a group of five children. They were wearing hard hats and were 'working' on a construction site, designing and building a house for the Three Billy Goats Gruff. They had a superb range of equipment from which to choose, including planks of various lengths and wooden blocks of different shapes and sizes. The teacher participated in their play, asking well phrased questions to develop and assess their understanding of shape, weight and length, such as 'Can you find a shorter plank than that one?' and 'Is it heavier than the other one or lighter'? She recorded the children's responses on a prepared sheet.

The activity was followed up well, using the interactive whiteboard and a program that showed pictures of different sized houses with three creatures of varying sizes alongside. The children were asked whether they thought the house would be better for the caterpillar, the dog or the giraffe, and were asked to explain why. All could offer good reasons: 'The giraffe's too tall, he wouldn't fit in'. 'It's a middle-sized house and the dog's middle-sized'. The children thoroughly enjoyed the activities, which also developed their gross motor skills, language, creative and social skills.

Other child-initiated activities included role play in the toy shop where children were pricing items and buying and selling them. They had the idea of using coins and giving change even though they did not fully understand the mathematics: 'Here's 1p'; 'Thank you – you need 1p back'.

From Ofsted (2009, p11)

Key stage 2 – Area of a shape

An example of a misconception in primary school mathematics, provided by Dawes (2005), is that when you double the size of a shape, the area will double. Dawes points out that this is based on the idea that in mathematics whatever happens on one side of an operation also happens on the other, but it could also just be that the pupils may regard it as 'common-sense'. In order to address this misconception the IWB and associated software can be very useful. For instance, by opening a page of squared paper and drawing a square 2x2 the whole class (or even to demonstrate to a group or individual) can count (or write numbers on the board, shade in squares using IWB pens or measure with a rule from the software tools) both the length of the sides and the number of squares within the shape. If this process is repeated with a shape 4x4 squares, it is easy to count again both the length of sides and the number of squares within the shape – provided of course that pupils understand the concept of area. With the IWB this process can be repeated as necessary with different size rectilinear shapes. Due to the features of ICT this can be done quickly, accurately and any results can be saved, printed or shared.

You may find the example of poor practice from Ofsted of interest in this context:

Weaker factors: gaps in subject knowledge	A Year 6 lesson on interior angles of polygons in which a teacher's weak subject knowledge led to pupils' incorrect understanding.
A Year 6 class was investigating the interior angles of regular polygons. Many found this difficult, but higher-attaining pupils had found that a pentagon has interior angles of 108 degrees. The teacher said that this was not correct and encouraged them to divide 360 degrees by 5 to get the answer, stating 'the angles in any polygon add up to 360 degrees'. This gave the answer of 72 degrees, which puzzled the most able pupils as the interior angles were clearly bigger than right angles. Other pupils appeared to just accept the rule which they then incorrectly applied to other polygons.	
How might it be improved?	The teacher had not realised that this was a gap in her knowledge. Possibly, she had confused previous knowledge about external angles which do sum to 360. If she had had the confidence to ask the able pupils to explain their answer, she might have recognised her error. She returned to the pupils' answer of 108 degrees in the next day's lesson.

From Ofsted (2009, p12)

ACTIVITY

Discus how the IWB and its tools could have helped to avoid this scenario.

Breadth of study

Hughes, Desforges and Mitchell (1999, p76) assert that 'children need to be taught from an early age how to apply their mathematical knowledge in a range of contexts and settings'. Therefore, the second area we must consider is how ICT can contribute to the breadth of study required in mathematics in the primary school. At present, in the National Curriculum (England) the breadth of study for mathematics at KS1 and 2 is shown in Table 7.1. Although this may vary as the curriculum is revised, and other national curricula may also vary, it serves as an indicative range of mathematical activities that we can consider.

Table 7.1 Breadth of Study – Mathematics Key Stages 1 and 2 (England)

Breadth of study	
KS1	**KS2**
Knowledge, skills and understanding 1. During the key stage, pupils should be taught the Knowledge, skills and understanding through: • practical activity, exploration and discussion • using mathematical ideas in practical activities, then recording these using objects, pictures, diagrams, words, numbers and symbols • using mental images of numbers and their relationships to support the development of mental calculation strategies • estimating, drawing and measuring in a range of practical contexts • drawing inferences from data in practical activities • **exploring and using a variety of resources and materials, including ICT** • activities that encourage them to make connections between number work and other aspects of their work in mathematics.	**Knowledge, skills and understanding** 1. During the key stage, pupils should be taught the Knowledge, skills and understanding through: • activities that extend their understanding of the number system to include integers, fractions and decimals • approximating and estimating more systematically in their work in mathematics • using patterns and relationships to explore simple algebraic ideas • applying their measuring skills in a range of contexts • drawing inferences from data in practical activities, and recognising the difference between meaningful and misleading representations of data • **exploring and using a variety of resources and materials, including ICT** • activities in which pupils decide when the use of calculators is appropriate and then use them effectively • using mathematics in their work in other subjects.

http://tinyurl.com/2wunt3h

Besides the explicit mention of ICT above, you need to consider how the features of ICT and particular pieces of hardware and software can help develop understanding of mathematics as a subject and address the require breadth of study above.

Like science in the next chapter, mathematics is a conceptual subject where learners need to progress from the observable to something much less tangible. Even apparently simple ideas like zero are in fact very difficult to understand (Cockburn and Littler, 2008). We have seen in earlier chapters that ICT can help to make visual, or model, ideas by using a variety of modes and media. In mathematics in the primary school, this is likely to become more useful as pupils progress from 'hands-on' practical work with real objects (manipulatives) to activities that cannot be solved by the manipulation of tangible objects. Manches (2006, p18) points out that there is a need to evaluate 'the potential for digital technologies to support learning in this area by enhancing such physical learning materials'. The advantages of doing this are outlined by Sarama and Clements (2009), who explore the benefits of using what they label 'computer manipulatives', that is, for instance, manipulating base-ten units on a computer or IWB compared to 'real' versions. A key idea here is that although 'physical concrete materials' may be needed to build meaning in the first instance, pupils then need be able to reflect on their actions. ICT provides the potential for pupils to do this by, for example, allowing them 'to explore geometric figures in ways that they cannot with physical shape sets. For example, children can change the size of the computer shapes, altering all shapes or only some'. (Sarama and Clements, 2009, p148)

WHAT DO YOU THINK?

A junior class was studying three-dimension shapes. The teacher put a collection of shapes on the tables of each group. The teacher introduced the lesson using a PowerPoint on the IWB. This gave the lesson objectives and then moved to a discussion about the properties of the shapes which the teacher showed on the IWB on successive slides. The shapes on the table remained untouched throughout this discussion. The teacher then used the IWB to show a scan of the actual worksheet, which the pupils then completed. The pupils were allowed to use the shapes if they required them when completing the sheet but, in reality, very few did as they had gained the information they needed from the IWB. The work was collected in for marking and the lesson ended with a whole class activity using a game from a website which covered properties of shapes.

As most of the pupils successfully completed the worksheet it could be argued that this was an effective use of technology. What do you think? What were the strengths and weaknesses of this approach?

Progression in mathematical thinking

Inherent in the discussion above is the ability of ICT to help with progression in mathematical thinking. One example of this could be in Key Stage 1, when pupils are required to use mathematical ideas 'in practical activities, then recording these using objects, pictures, diagrams, words, numbers and symbols' (f. in Table 7.1, p106). Such a progression, perhaps over a period of years, might involve counting the numbers of toy ducks, pigs and chickens (tangible objects), to drawing a pictogram (representation of the real object) as a class activity (on the IWB using software with data input by the teacher), then children constructing pictograms on laptop, then a bar chart (using abstract data input by the pupils in a more complicated program such as Excel), through to the manipulation of data in dynamic graphing software to explore the effect of changing variables (done by pupils on the IWB to explore their own ideas with the whole class). The time taken for this progression will vary and be guided by the developmental stage of members of the class rather than their age. While you may be planning each part of this progression it is necessary to remember that the 'baseline' (an assessment of the starting point of knowledge or experience) will be different for individual pupils and one extreme would be that all of these stages may be represented by levels of development in one class! Another example in Key Stage 2, is when pupils are required to undertake activities 'that extend their understanding of the number system to include integers, fractions and decimals' (a. in Table 7.1 above). Early work on fractions may include practical work with real objects, such as cutting up fruit or a cake. In developing this concept the IWB can be useful in moving to annotating representations of the fruit or cake, through to the symbolic representation and dragging and dropping activities using matching symbolic and pictorial representations. (There is another dimension here – or lack of it! – as we move from 3D shapes to 2D representations so you need to be sure pupils understand this conceptual step.)

Although not all the breadth of study can, or even should, use ICT, the IWB in particular does allow you to model what is required in subsequent activities, such as using the ruler or protractor built into most IWB software for demonstrating how to measure. Although pupil could undertake similar work on the IWB, it is really a tool for the teacher to ensure pupils understand the task before they use real measuring equipment in practical work.

Number

As the purpose of this book is to consider pedagogy using ICT, we will not consider a list of 'how to' activities, but we will consider how ICT can contribute to the development of understanding number. Central to this process is the exploration of what ICT can offer that will enhance the existing learning environment. Such an approach is based on an acceptance of Yelland and Kilderry's (2010, p95) belief that 'new technologies or ICT can provide different opportunities for thinking about and extending the teaching and learning of mathematical skills and processes'. They continue to assert that ICT is most likely to be used effectively in multidimensional mathematical tasks which 'are characterised by the students having greater autonomy in terms of the amount of input that they have into the direction of their learning'. (p101) This is in contrast to a unidimensional mathematical task which 'is characterised by simple sequences of activity that often have a single outcome, minimal opportunities for exploration and where mathematical concepts and processes are introduced via structured tasks'. (p97) ICT can be used in both of these approaches, but the multidimensional approach reflects the interactive and dialogic strategies discussed in earlier chapters and is more likely to result in creative use of technology, and hence new opportunities for learning. It is necessary to point out that such an approach does not mean the exclusive use of ICT, but rather the selective use (by the pupils). In reality, it is suggested that the mastery of 'basic' skills is likely to be achieved by unidimensional tasks, but this should not be at the expense of exploring their use in multidimensional tasks – particularly by using number work (or other areas of mathematics) in, for example, problem-solving cross-curricular work.

This discussion does not rule out using ICT to present existing parts of the environment in new ways. Indeed, this can be a very effective use of ICT. For instance, Hughes, Desforges and Mitchell (1999) outline a scenario in Key Stage 1 where a teacher gave two pupils a series of pieces of cards with either a sign or number on it, e.g. 2, 5, 7, +, – and =. They were asked to explore how they could be arranged 'to make them work together'. The outcomes included 7 – 5 = 2 and 5 + 2 = 7. The outcomes were then discussed between teacher and pupils. It is not difficult to see that this activity could easily become a drag and drop activity on the IWB, but the fundamental difference would be the speed that resources could be retrieved and used – not to mention the saving of card! In the ICT scenario, the teacher could have a flip chart already prepared with an example on the first page to introduce the idea to the class, but his could be followed by a series of pages within the same file with differentiated sets of numbers for different groups of pupils to work on, finishing with a final page with a plenary activity on. If the pupils use the IWB as a resource for the activity on a rotation (annotating the relevant page with their names using the pen tool), all outcomes can be discussed (reviewed) with the whole class or other groups as required, before being saved as evidence for assessment. Extension activity can also be undertaken as the pupils are able easily to add their own numbers and signs to their page – or the teacher could have them already prepared on later pages. Similar principles apply to other number work such sequencing, ordering and sorting activities.

ACTIVITY

Discuss how you could use the approach outlined above in sequencing, ordering and sorting activities. Either on your own, or with others, plan a lesson based on one of these and decide how and when ICT could be used effectively, exploiting the relevant features of ICT.

In the discussion above, an existing idea has been adapted effectively to use ICT in number work. We must know consider how *different* opportunities for thinking about and extending the teaching and learning of mathematical skills and processes can be achieved.

Shape, space and measure

As we have already said above, the IWB has a range of tools (such as rulers and protractors) built into most IWB software (free with boards), but these are likely to be tools for the teacher to model tasks – such as reading rulers when not the whole number. It is suggested that shape, space and measure are areas where practical activities with real rulers is much better than using ICT. However, this does not mean that ICT has no role, but this role needs to be selective. For instance, Serow and Callingham (2011, p170) suggest that a mixture of group work involving 'constructions with concrete materials, electronic geoboard constructions, and written recording of known properties and relationships of shapes seemed effective in focussing students on the mathematics'. The ability to manipulate shapes and angles in 2D is a strength of the IWB and other software packages on laptops or computers, so this may be a good use of ICT, whereas for 3D shapes, real shapes may be best.

When recording the results of investigations, however, ICT becomes a very good option, particularly if pupils have access to mobile devices and can therefore begin to not only record, but also analyse results both inside and outside of school. In addition, digital photographs of the objects being measured may be useful in reporting back to the class about what a particular group did.

Handling data

One of the strengths of ICT is in handling data and, in one sense, computers represent a manipulative for this area of study. In planning work in this area, it is necessary to remember that, although explicit direct teaching may be needed in early stages of learning skills, wherever possible the National Curriculum requires that 'teaching should ensure that appropriate connections are made between the sections on 'number', 'shape, space and measures', and 'handling data'. To achieve this, it is likely that data will be considered in the context of cross-curricular activities where data is encountered in authentic contexts (or at least as authentic as possible within the framework of the activities), so that the results of handling data have a meaning or application. The main advantages of ICT in handling data are speed and the ability to explore ideas (provisionality and automaticity). For instance, it is quite possible, and indeed necessary at times, for pupils to construct their own graphs with paper and pencil, but ICT can do it much quicker. In addition, having constructed graphs, ICT also allows variables to be changed with instant and observable changes in graphs. Even the type of graph can be changed instantly to see which type it best suited to the purpose of the activity.

Calculators

Although calculators are a form of ICT, this is not really the place to discuss their role in any detail except to note that the features of ICT that apply are speed and provisionality.

SUMMARY

Overall, academic research in the area of primary mathematics and ICT is much less common than in secondary schools. In 1999, Higgins and Muuijs (1999) suggested that the emphasis on research in mathematics to date had been on CAI (Computer Assisted Instruction) and CAL (Computer Aided Learning), with most work concentrating on secondary schools or post-secondary education. More recently, there has been research on the influence on the IWB in mathematics, but this has again mainly focussed largely on secondary schools (e.g. Miller and Glover, 2007). We have seen that ICT, particularly the IWB, can play an important role in developing the teaching of mathematics in the primary school from an early age. As in earlier chapters, the most important concern is to only use ICT when it offers something that no other resources can, or does it quicker or more efficiently. As such, digital technologies should be used as interconnected environments, rather than unrelated tools, for learning. Way and Beardon (2003) suggest that in mathematics teaching (and perhaps more generally) there is a major difference between these two perspectives that require teachers to fundamentally change the way they teach. It is hoped that, if you have read this far, you will not need to change too much!

References

Cockburn, A. and Littler, G. (eds) (2008), *Mathematical Misconceptions*, London: Sage.

Eagle, S., Manches, A., O'Malley, C., Plowman, L. and Sutherland, R. (2006), *From Research to Design: Perspectives on Early Years and Digital Technologies*, Bristol: Futurelab.

Hughes, M., Desforges, C. and Mitchell, C. (1999), 'Using and applying mathematics at Key Stage 1', in Thompson, I. (ed.), Issues in Teaching Numeracy in Primary Schools, Buckingham: Open University Press.

Manches, A. (2006), 'What can the digital add to physical learning materials in early years numeracy classrooms?' in Eagle et al., (2006), pp18–32.

Miller, D. and Glover, D. (2007), 'Into the unknown: the professional development induction experience of secondary mathematics teachers using interactive white-board technology', *Learning, Media and Technology*, 32: 3, 319–31.

Murphy, C. (2006), 'Why do we have to do this?' Primary trainee teachers' views of a subject knowledge audit in mathematics, *British Educational Research Journal*, 32:02, 227–50.

Nunes, T. (2001), 'British research on the development of numeracy concepts', in Askew, M. and Brown, M., *Teaching and Learning Primary Numeracy: Policy, Practice and Effectiveness: A Review of British Research for the British Educational Research Association in Conjunction with the British Society for Research in the Learning of Mathematics*, pp1–14.

OFSTED (2009), *Mathematics: Understanding the Score: Improving Practice in Mathematics Teaching at Primary Level*, London: OFSTED.

O'Malley, C. and Stanton Fraser, D, (2000). *Literature Review in Learning with Tangible Technologies*, Bristol: Futurelab.

Serow, P. and Callingham, R. (2011), 'Levels of use of interactive whiteboard technology in the primary mathematics classroom'. *Technology, Pedagogy and Education*, 20:2, 161–73.

Further reading

OFSTED (2009), *Mathematics: Understanding the Score: Improving Practice in Mathematics Teaching at Primary Level*, London: OFSTED.

ICT in Cross Curricular Teaching at Key Stages 1 and 2

In this chapter we will consider how teachers can use the range and the features of technology outlined in earlier chapters in powerful and empowering ways in the classroom for leaners aged 5–11. We will consider the distinction between ICT's use both within and across subjects and explore how viewing learning objectives through a variety of subject 'lenses' can help to provide new ways of planning lessons for teachers and new ways of using ICT for pupils.

The curriculum context

In the current National Curriculum in England, and other countries, ICT exists as a separate subject, but there is also an explicit expectation that it should also be used across the curriculum in the primary school. Whilst details may vary between countries, and even change with each new government, the main point is that ICT has two purposes. As Hall (2010) points out, all pupils have an entitlement to develop [individual] skills, but they also need to use them to enhance learning across the curriculum. In this chapter we will consider how ICT can be used effectively to enhance a range of subjects, but also how subject 'lenses' can lead to new ways to use ICT for both teachers and pupils (Beauchamp, 2010). We have seen in previous chapters that such an approach is in line with a more pupil-focused, rather than subject-focused, pedagogy. If pupils are able to try and solve, for instance, a mathematics problem by examining it from a variety of perspectives (using ICT as appropriate), they are more likely to be both motivated and able to find a range of possible solutions. These different perspectives, or lenses, will be examined in more detail below but we must first consider the 'official' view of how ICT should be used across the curriculum, before moving to examine other approaches.

In England, in addition to specific subject requirements for ICT, pupils should also:

> *be given opportunities to apply and develop their ICT capability through the use of ICT tools to support their learning in all subjects. At key stage 1, it is statutory to teach the use of ICT in English, mathematics and science. Teachers should use their own judgement to decide where it is appropriate across these subjects. At other key stages, there are statutory requirements to use ICT in all statutory subjects, except PE.*
>
> *Pupils should be given opportunities to support their work by being taught to:*
>
> - *find things out from a variety of sources, selecting and synthesising the information to meet their needs and developing an ability to question its accuracy, bias and plausibility*

- *develop their ideas using ICT tools to amend and refine their work and enhance its quality and accuracy*
- *exchange and share information, both directly and through electronic media*
- *review, modify and evaluate their work, reflecting critically on its quality, as it progresses.*

(http://tinyurl.com/44l9zeh)

Another example, from the curriculum in Wales, includes a less prescriptive, but no less inclusive, expectation of 'skills across the curriculum' is that

> *Learners develop their ICT skills across the curriculum by finding, developing, creating and presenting information and ideas and by using a wide range of equipment and software. Learners use ICT individually and collaboratively, depending on the nature and context of the task in hand.*

(http://tinyurl.com/3rsv9ky)

These official expectations demonstrate the range of possible uses of ICT, but they also demonstrate that this is a developmental process. As we have seen elsewhere, although pupils may have freedom to explore ICT uses in a heuristic manner, there is also an expectation that the teacher provides the structure and potential for such actions, as well as ensuring they have the necessary technical skills. At the same time, teachers need to ensure that they are encouraging a critical perspective about ICT use on the part of pupils. The same applies to ICT use on the part of the teacher and there is evidence that teachers do make these distinctions across the curriculum. (Beauchamp, 2011)

Categories of interaction in the primary school

It is particularly important in cross-curricular teaching that pupils are given a range of experiences, in a variety of places. To help with seeing how ICT may fit into this range of experiences I have suggested elsewhere (Beauchamp, 2011) that a possible framework for planning in the primary school is provided by the categories below:

- physical dialogic interaction: learners with resources;
- located interaction: learners with classroom setting, place/physical community;
- community interaction: learners with peers, teachers and other adults;
- technology-mediated interaction: learners with ICT.

Each of these categories can be used individually, but also in combination; for example, different groups doing different activities for one lesson or moving between categories within a lesson. From the above you will notice that ICT-mediated interaction is only one possible approach, thus encouraging the selective use of ICT advocated in earlier chapters. To help make some sense of these categories, and their possible use, we will examine each one briefly before moving to consider their context in cross-curricular teaching.

Physical dialogic interaction: learners with resources

In this category, work across the curriculum is conducted using a range of (non-ICT) resources. As I have written elsewhere, 'the planned use of resources is not new to the primary classroom. Indeed, planning how to use them is central to all teacher-training courses. What distinguishes their use in the context of interactive teaching is the specific intention to use them to stimulate dialogue and debate rather than being an end in itself; a situation where learning is the result of the dialogue, as much as the use of the resource'. (Beauchamp, 2011, p181) This dialogue is based on the dialogic principles we have examined elsewhere (see Chapter 2). This category would include the use of manipulatives in mathematics (for instance money in a Key Stage 1 shop), but also anything from a mini wipe-clean whiteboard to a fossil or dressing-up box. In general terms, in the primary school the function of the resource, and the nature of the interaction, become more explicit the older the class being taught. This is especially the case in the use of subject-specific resources, such as the digital microscope in science.

Located interaction: learners with classroom setting and place/physical community

In this category there are two distinct, but related settings (learners with classroom setting and learners with place/physical community) and we will discuss each below.

Learners with classroom setting

Primary classrooms come in many shapes and sizes and this is bound to have an impact on how pupils and teachers interact. A central feature of this category is the view that the classroom itself is considered a teaching resource and parts of it are the subject of planned interactions. Although perhaps more obvious in Key Stage 1 and Early Years classrooms, located interactions can take place across the primary school with classroom displays, both on wall-mounted boards and surfaces, or 'zones'. Evidence from a research project suggests that

> *some classrooms provide small discrete areas for discussion in groups, others provide large open spaces with easy access for pupils (and teachers) to move around and interact or hold whole-class discussions, whilst others still (such as an L-shaped classroom in one school) make interactions much more challenging. This architecture-shaped discourse is a factor that teachers need to consider when planning lessons, but is not always a negative feature.*
> *(Beauchamp, 2011, p182)*

These more unusual classroom, or school, layouts can be helpful to provide a variety of working areas for groups or individuals not possible in more open-plan settings. The interactions in this category can be between pupils and features of the setting, such as a mathematics table, but can also include the IWB. In this context, the IWB is considered a feature of the setting (chosen for use as such, for instance for a group to record their thoughts on a problem on an *ad hoc* basis because it was to hand), not a mediating ICT resource.

Learners with place/physical community

Having made the decision to move outside of the classroom setting, teachers make explicit choices about what the location can supply in terms of personal, physical or even emotional stimuli. This is particularly true when the size or context of the setting (for example a church or historical site, such as a prehistoric cave) add something unique to the learning experience, something that could not be created using ICT. Some areas of the curriculum, such as Religious Education or history, may present more obvious choices for place/community interactions, but opportunities in other areas of the curriculum should not be neglected. One of the most important aspects of this category is the opportunity to work in a cross-curricular way and ICT has a role in facilitating and recording such events. Indeed, it may be that once in the setting the interactions change to technology-mediated interactions – see below.

CASE STUDY

A class of Y3 children are working with an educator from the local museum. He takes them on a trip to a prehistoric cave situated some miles from their school in the countryside. Prior to the trip the pupils have worked on musical compositions and are confident in working collaboratively with the educator. On the trip the class is split into groups with some visiting other historical sites close by and one group visit the prehistoric cave. The groups are rotated throughout the day. In common with the concept of 'strangely familiar' discussed later, one of the aims of the visit was to encourage pupils to listen with fresh ears (Shafer, 1994) by removing them from the classroom and putting them in an environment which added something unique. As one of the pupils reported in interviews after the visit, it was different because 'cavemen lived in that actual cave you just feel that their spirits are still there … and you like come to life!' (Adams, 2011) Once in the cave the pupils improvised some compositions reflecting the mood invoked by the cave and its history. This was recorded by a digital recorder for later appraisal (a component of the National Curriculum where the study was undertaken – the discussion of music using musical 'language' and terms) in the classroom. Another important feature to note from this case study is that as well as an emotional response, the setting was also be able to invoke other responses based on the particular features of the setting such as size, sound qualities or quality of light. In this case, Adams (2011) reports that it was the sound qualities of the cave which the children noted and offered a unique level, and type, of feedback they had not experienced in the school setting. They reported that:

- When we were sitting down you could actually feel the vibration of the music on the floor of the cave. You could feel the beat of the music!
- They were good vibrations … because I haven't ever felt my music before!
- It felt like a herd of elephants jumping on the floor! The vibration made you want to move and to dance!

In this example we see that although technology was used, and provided a convenient, accurate and quick way of capturing the moment (which would otherwise have been ephemeral), the main focus was on the interaction between the learners with the particular features and nature of the place.

Community interaction: learners with peers, teachers and other adults

In this category, teachers make a distinction between the physical setting that a community (class) works in (as above) and the setting as a community of practice (Wenger, 1998). The role of the teacher is to make interactions possible in a 'community of enquiry', which include Wenger's (1998, p. 72) 'three dimensions of the relationship by which practice is the source of coherence of a community': mutual engagement, a joint enterprise and a shared repertoire. In the primary school, with mainly one teacher for each class, this type of community is much easier to establish than, for instance, in secondary schools. This type of community is exemplified by the language that teachers use in describing their classroom and how it works. One example from a recent research project (cited in Beauchamp, 2011) will serve to demonstrate how this works in a cross-curricular context:

> *each area of the classroom obviously is themed, you've got your doing table, your writing area, your sand table, you know the different areas and we try and contextualise it all, so this week we're doing spiders. On the gluing table we are making spiders, cutting out little bits of paper and different materials and they're sticking bits on spiders. On the art table we are going to do weaving in and out on card with spiders. Painting will be spider webs, our literacy time this week is on rhymes about spiders like Little Miss Muffet, Incy Wincey. The Science table has got books on spiders in the reading corner and we've got a bug house in the role play corner.*

In this quote the consistent use of the word 'we' represents a level of mutual engagement and joint enterprise that, allied to effective classroom organisation, will lead to a shared repertoire of language, activities and routines. It could be argued that this approach pervades primary teaching, and it is hoped that, when combined with an interactive dialogic pedagogy, this community interaction facilitates a high level of engagement from pupils and teachers. It is also suggested that with shared understanding of routines and language, pupils will be in a better position to become active co-constructors of their own knowledge. In this context, it is necessary to ensure that the 'shared repertoire' includes ICT skills on the part of both pupil and teacher.

Having examined three categories of interaction that are not reliant on the features of ICT, we will now consider what ICT can add.

Technology-mediated interaction: learners with ICT

In this category, technology (mainly ICT) is a 'mediating artifact' (Engeström, 2001) in the learning process. Sometimes the interactions are planned and instigated by the teacher, but they can also be where the technology is used 'to mediate interactions between learners in a manner not predicted by the teacher'. (Beauchamp, 2011, p184) As distinct from the use of the IWB as a feature of the setting above, in this category the IWB would be chosen not just because it was there, but specifically for its ability to offer a way of communicating or exploring (mediating) ideas in a variety of ways which exploit the features of ICT. An important feature of this category is the sheer variety of interactions that ICT can facilitate. If the IWB, classroom PCs or mobile devices have an internet connection we have already seen that this can mediate interactions between pupils not only within the school, but also anywhere in the world with the requisite facilities. In addition, as we have seen in earlier chapters, with mobile devices (such as ipods) pupils can also record and share thoughts in a variety of modes and media.

It is important to reiterate that the categories above are used by teachers in combination or in sequence and are not necessarily the basis for whole lessons.

ICT across the curriculum

This potential for ICT across the curriculum is outlined by Becta (2002, p2) who suggest that

> *ICT gives pupils immediate access to richer source materials. Multimedia can present problems from real life which draw on the previous learning and experience of pupils and link it to their current learning. Using e-mail, pupils can engage in 'authentic' communications. In modern foreign languages for example, CD-ROM and interactive video allow pupils to interact with original source materials and on-line experts in new ways that can lead to more reflective work and deeper understanding. Data-logging equipment can be used in and outside of the classroom in conjunction with portables. Pupils can then input this data into spreadsheets and databases and represent it in a number of ways. Digital and video cameras can also be used to record field trips. This gives pupils experience of 'hands on' data collection and helps identify the practical application of ICT in the real world. Computer simulations also allow children to experience a variety of realistic experiences without risk.*

This list of possibilities only hints at the full range of ICT use across the curriculum. In an integrated approach, ICT is seen not just as a tool for a particular subject, but as a means of integrating subjects in a cross-curricular approach to teaching. This is important if we agree with Barnes (2007:1) that 'our experience of the world is cross-curricular. Everything which surrounds us in the physical world can be seen and understood from multiple perspectives'. One of these perspectives may be that of a scientist, geographer or historian and here the challenges begin in framing learning experiences for children in the primary school. I have written elsewhere that 'each subject gives a child a unique way of understanding the world and that viewing teaching ideas through, for example, a 'scientific lens', can offer new insights into how to develop effective learning opportunities'. (Beauchamp, 2010, p169–170) In this situation the particular 'lens', or combination of 'lenses', adopted would predominantly be decided by the teacher in the first instance, but this may well change as children develop their own ideas. Bennett et al., (2007, p12) suggest that 'children finding out about their environment do not consciously signal changes in their thinking as they ask 'geographical' questions about their locality or 'scientific' questions about their environment, or use 'mathematical' or 'ICT' skills to measure and record'. Perhaps this is true of the very early years in primary school, but as children progress they are aware that, for example, mathematicians need to work carefully and accurately and that scientists need to observe carefully. It is this context that the idea of subject lenses is proposed. It may well be that this operates at two levels (one for the teacher thinking of possible approaches to planning, the other for children thinking of ways to approach a problem), but the key idea is that you consider the possible benefits of approaching teaching and learning as, say, a musician or historian.

The does not mean teaching a 'subject', but adopting a methodology appropriate to that subject to view the task through its lens. This allows something to become what Barnes and Shirley (2007) call 'strangely familiar'. They suggest that 'even familiar aspects of life could be looked upon as unfamiliar and that the new could be seen as unthreatening'. (p164) By looking at familiar topics through a different subject 'lens', as well as its own, it is suggested that new approaches and dimensions of the problem can be seen, which might provoke novel teaching approaches and solutions by both the teacher and the pupils.

To explore this approach further, let us consider history as an example. We are not interested in teaching just historical subject knowledge (for example historical 'facts', such as the year of a particular battle – although 'drill' exercises or games on a computer cold do this or reinforce this), but rather looking at the problems as an historian – even if the subject is not history. Turner-Bisset (2005) suggests the following processes of enquiry are appropriate for primary school 'historians':

- *Searching for evidence*
- *Examining the evidence*
- *Recording of accounts*
- *Summarising historical narrative or argument.*

From what we have seen in earlier chapters it should be apparent that ICT can have a role in each of these processes. Examples of using this in science are shown in Table 8.1 where a Y5 class search the school grounds for plants. The class work in groups looking for different plants and then report back at the end – see over page.

ACTIVITY

Using the headings below make a list of how ICT can help in each process for your chosen age phase/range in a range of subjects across the curriculum.

Subject/ area	Searching for evidence	Examining the evidence	Recording of accounts	Summarising (historical) narrative or argument.

In undertaking the activity above you may have noticed that some of these processes are also used in other subjects. For example, with a slight rewording of the final process, all of these items are part of the process skills in science. Harlen and Qualter (2004, p66) suggest that in primary school science (the science lens) children begin to develop the listed on the next page skills and attitudes:

Table 8.1 Using historical processes of enquiry in another subject

Subject/ area of learning	Searching for evidence	Examining the evidence	Recording of accounts	Summarising historical narrative or argument.
Science	• using the internet to research a plant – where it might be found ...	• taking pictures of habitat were it was found • looking at leaves with a digital microscope and magnifying glasses	• taking pictures of actual plant from variety of angles and using zoom with digital camera • use digital recorder (or mobile device) to interview other members of the group about where the plant was found, what it looked like *in situ* and any other relevant factors • write notes on a laptop and save interview sound files	• preparing and delivering a short presentation for the class using internet research, pictures from, words and sound files of interview in a PowerPoint presentation using the IWB

Process (enquiry) skills

- questioning, predicting and planning;
- gathering evidence by observing and using information sources;
- interpreting evidence and drawing conclusions;
- communicating and reflecting.

ACTIVITY

Using the headings in the bullet points above make a list of how ICT can help in each process for your chosen age phase/range. Then compare and contrast with previous activity. What conclusions do you draw about the use of ICT?

In addition, Harlen and Qualter (2004) outline scientific attitudes that may also apply to other areas of the curriculum:

1. Willingness to consider evidence and change ideas;
2. Sensitivity to living things and the environment.

Another feature of using a scientific lens is the way that scientists assess and address misconceptions. Much work was done on this area in science by the SPACE (Science Process And Concept Exploration Project ,1991) and CLISP (Children's Learning In Science Project, 1984–1991) – but other studies exist in areas such as mathematics – see Chapter 7. In previous chapters we have seen that ICT can present ideas in a wide variety of forms. As such, it may be that ICT can be very useful in presenting challenges to current concepts, in a variety of areas of the curriculum, that may provoke a fundamental rethink – hopefully towards a more 'correct' conception! It is perhaps easiest to consider this in a three-stage process:

1. Assessing and recording current conceptions and/or misconceptions;
2. Presenting alternative perspectives;
3. Assessing and recording new conceptions (and new misconceptions!).

As this is a cycle, we will consider the first two below, with the assumption that the principles of the first will also apply for the third.

Assessing and recording current conceptions and/or misconceptions – Assessment with ICT

McDougall (2001) makes the important distinction between 'assessing *learning with ICT*'(how ICT affects learning) and *'assessing learning* with ICT' (using ICT to assess learning). We have already discussed the first of these in chapter 1 (see Cox et al., 2003) and the latter briefly in Chapter 7 when discussing specialised testing software CAL and CAI. What we must now consider is how more generic ICT resources can be helpful in using ICT to assess learning. As there are many books already which cover different modes of assessment (such as diagnostic, formative, summative, norm-referenced, criterion-referenced, ipsative and so on) in detail, we will assume that decisions about which mode of assessment to be used have already been made and will deal with generic principles of how they work with ICT. In other words, what unique strategies of assessment can ICT offer in addition to more established methods?

When making assessments we need to consider two broad categories, which in research terms might be called pre- and post-activity assessments. In other words what the pupils know before the teaching and what they know afterwards.

Assessing existing understanding with ICT

This apparently simple concept, however, is not as straightforward as it may seem as pupils rarely have complete understanding but a series of connected ideas, some of which are 'right' and some 'wrong'. Some form of broad, but nuanced, criteria are needed. Summers, Kruger and Mant (1998, p157) provide a useful framework for pre-teaching assessments in science, but this could equally be applied to other areas of the curriculum. They suggest teachers could look for:

- *preconceptions* – either a misconception, that is, a scientifically incorrect idea, or a partially understood scientific idea;
- *missing* – a scientific idea for which there was no evidence of any knowledge or understanding;
- *knows* – a scientific idea of which the child demonstrated knowledge and understanding.

In making such judgements you could use a range of practical activities with no ICT, and it may well be possible to identify the level of the pupil's understanding using questioning, written tests or practical tasks. In addition, assessments can sometimes be made in unexpected situation, such as in a class discussion.

ACTIVITY

You are talking to your class, in this case Key Stage 2, about what they did over the weekend and it becomes obvious that one child in your (chosen age range) thinks that the moon is a source of light. The pupil has heard it in stories and their mum took them for a 'walk in the moonlight' last weekend as it was a full moon – which the child tells you means that there was 'more light as the moon was bigger'. The child has dyslexia and is not keen on writing. How could you use ICT to support this child in explaining why they think that: 1.) the moon makes light and 2.) the moon is bigger?

What we need to consider is what the features of ICT can add to this. In this context, the IWB can be a useful tool. When used in an interactive way as discussed earlier, it helps to make explicit, things which may have been internalised without ICT, as pupils share ideas or articulate their thinking. As Beauchamp and Kennewell (2008, p311) propose, 'the communal nature of the IWB, combined with the culture of valuing mistakes for their learning potential, may have facilitated the exposure of pupils' misconceptions. Many pupils were encouraged to articulate their thinking about key ideas and evaluate the viability of alternative perspectives'. Such an approach is very helpful for helping teachers to assess (in real time and afterwards) and record (by saving) pupils' current ideas. This is not to say that the same thing cannot be done using more traditional resource, but as Beauchamp and Kennewell (2008, p312) continue to report, teachers feel that the IWB is able to give 'better support for reflection than manual tools – particularly through sharing ideas with the whole class … , displaying pupils' work and reviewing what was done on the board earlier in the lesson'.

Assessing understanding after teaching with ICT

Having undertaken teaching activities it is also necessary to check the level of understanding. Summers, Kruger and Mant (1998, p157) provide the following post-teaching classifications for this process which they suggest can be matched to the pre-teaching ideas:

- ideas:
- successfully acquired;
- partially acquired;
- incorrectly acquired;
- not acquired;
- unchanged ideas.

In making such judgements the same features of working with the IWB will apply. Depending on the level of understanding above, the teacher will then decide on the next course of action in how to present alternative perspectives and what form these perspectives need to take.

Presenting alternative perspectives

Having established *what* pupils think, and *why* they think it, you then need consider how this can be addressed and how big or small the next steps will be. At the same time you need to decide if ICT can contribute in any way, or is not needed at all – the guiding principle being 'does ICT do it better than anything else'?

The example of moonlight above was deliberately chosen as something which is apparently simple, but in reality is very complex, with many related challenging concepts (such as planetary motion) that need to be understood to address the original concept or idea. It may even be that you cannot address the main issue at all (at least in the short term), as there are so many underlying misconceptions that need to be dealt with first or, perhaps more cynically, that it is not in the curriculum, or the school scheme of work for your year group, so need not be addressed. (How do you feel about this latter argument?) A full understanding of what pupils think of all related concepts is important (if time consuming) and tracking back through underlying conceptions to see where the misconception begins is a vital part of understanding why children think as they do and how it may be changed. To do this, however, your own understanding of relevant concepts needs to be as complete as possible in all subject areas (which is the role of subject knowledge in primary teaching) and ICT can help with this as well.

Having established an area where you wish to represent ideas, and having made the decision that ICT is the best way to do it (because it can do something better than anything else), you are faced with a number of options based on one or more of the features of ICT explored in earlier chapters. In each case, however, you need to decide why ICT is better. To help frame this we will look at an example from science, based on Summers, Kruger and Mant (1998), which may be useful to set you thinking. Two scenarios are outlined below that focus on understanding the flow of electricity in a circuit. Both use an analogy to help teach the following key ideas:

- the battery as 'pusher' of electrons
- the electrons (already in the wire) all start moving at the same time
- the electrons move in the same direction all around the circuit and are not produced by the battery
- the strength of the battery is a measure of its 'push'

In this analogy the pedals represent the battery and the links in the chain are the electrons. The class have done some work on circuits already (to make a bulb light up) but in this work it became clear that they did not really understand the flow of electricity. The teacher decides to address this specifically and decides to use an analogy to help.

Scenario A: The teacher uses the IWB to show the class a video of an upturned bike (with the chain clearly visible). At the start of the video the pedals are still. Through open questioning, the teacher establishes that the children understand what this represents (e.g. pedals/battery; chain links/electrons; wheel hub/bulb) and the relative state of each (e.g. no current, electrons are present but not moving around circuit). The teacher then plays the video and the pedals are turned. The teacher pauses the video and asks the children to look carefully at the chain and pedals – to focus attention on important features to avoid possible misconceptions. Again, the teacher plays the video and uses open questions to ask what is happening now (battery 'pushing' electrons in one direction around the circuit). The teacher minimises the video and uses the IWB flipchart software to ask a child to show the picture left and discusses what it represents. The teacher asks for a volunteer to label the picture and draw arrows around the 'circuit' to show the direction the electrons are travelling. The teacher then resumes the video in which the pedals are now turned faster. After pausing the video, the teacher resumes open questions to see if pupils understand that the strength of the battery is a measure of its 'push'. The teacher then minimises the video and returns to the IWB software and goes to next page in the flipchart which shows the following picture. This is then discussed and the teacher asks for a volunteer to label and draw direction of flow of electrons. The class then discuss what makes the current flow and introduce the notion of the person pedalling acting as a switch. Having addressed the aims of the analogy, the teacher then returns to practical work and the next areas of learning in this area.

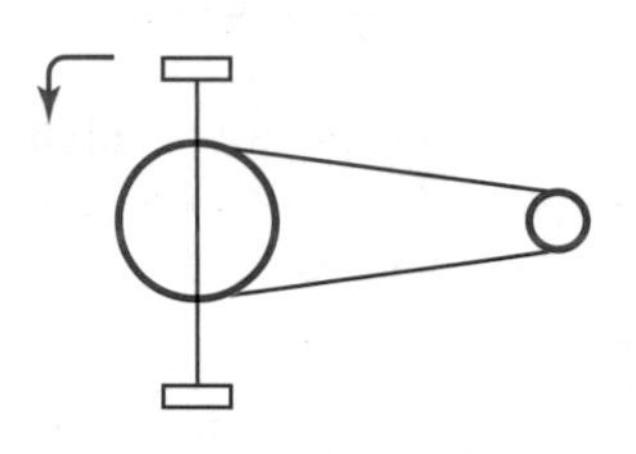

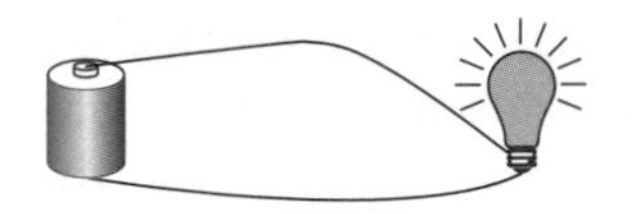

Scenario B: In this scenario, the teacher brings a real bike into the classroom and turns it upside down on the table. The teacher moves the class around the bike and, through open questioning, establishes that the children understand what this represents (e.g. pedals/battery; chain links/electrons; wheel hub/bulb) and the relative state of each (e.g. no current, electrons are present but not moving around circuit). The teacher then asks for a volunteer to turn the pedals and the lesson progresses as 1 above but the teacher has to draw the pictures on a whiteboard as there is no IWB. A second volunteer is used to turn the pedals faster.

ACTIVITY

Even if the teacher in scenario 2 had an IWB, what are the benefits of each of the above? Which approach would you use and why?

Challenge 1: In the discussion one pupil points out that the 'electrons' (chain) are going around the 'bulb' (wheel hub) and therefore asks how they can light it? How do you respond? *Key idea: this is only an analogy – refer to diagram.*

Challenge 2: Another pupil points out that when you stop pedalling (battery), the wheel will keep moving. They compare this to the bulb and ask will it stay alight? *Key idea: although the wheel is moving the electrons (chain) are not – the wheel is not the bulb.*

It is likely, however, that teachers will use a mixture of ICT and non-ICT resources in the classroom as demonstrated in the case study below:

CASE STUDY

A Y5 class are studying 'Forces' in science. The class teacher decided that she wants the class to have practical experience with tangible objects. The practical activity involves running a toy car down a ramp and changing the angle of the ramp to see the effect on the distance travelled – the only variable changed was the angle of the ramp to ensure a fair test. There was only one ramp so the teacher made the pragmatic decision to use this with a group and rotate the groups so that all pupils undertake the practical activity during the lesson. The teacher decided that the other groups can do a mixture of revision and research activities related to the topic 'Forces', some aspects of which they had already covered in earlier years. One group did research on laptops using a science CD-ROM (as they had no wireless connection) to answer questions on a worksheet. Another group used the IWB to play a game of 'Who wants to be a Millionaire' about forces, which the teacher had prepared using a PowerPoint template. In this group one person asked the questions and used the IWB pen to advance the slides whilst the rest of the group were put into pairs to answer the questions – the teacher had told the pupils their partner in advance to ensure mixed-ability groupings. They recorded the scores on a paper flip chart next to the IWB. One group worked with a classroom assistant on unrelated reading activities which were scheduled throughout the week. The final group worked with the class teacher on the practical science activity with the ramp and toy car. The teacher wanted to ensure that the correct conceptions were developed and that appropriate science language was used correctly. When the teacher was satisfied that they understood, the pupils in this group had to record their findings in their science books together with

(continued)

a record of the investigation using a writing frame they were familiar with. The class teacher rotated the groups so that all had covered all activities during the course of the lesson.

At the end of the lesson the teacher gave the whole class individual voting devices connected to the IWB. A series of questions were asked relating to the work that had been covered and after everyone had voted the teacher discussed the answers based on the percentage of correct or incorrect answers. The software related to the voting devices also gave the teacher an individual record of responses for records. This voting was very quick and the pupils, who had used the devices on previous occasions, were very engaged in the questions.

ACTIVITY

In the final whole class voting session in the case study above, we come across two issues which can apply to all use of ICT:

- it is possible to guess the correct answer and;
- sometimes pupils try to be the first to answer so they forsake accuracy for speed.

How could you avoid this in your lessons?

Other subject lenses

Having seen some examples from science, let us also look at how ICT and subject lenses may work in other areas, beginning with a study of a location using a variety of geography lenses.

Location

In examining a location it is necessary to recognise that pupils 'are citizens of their localities, making contributions to their communities whether playing sport, interacting with others or simply 'hanging out' with friends ... [and they] have views about the past, present and future of their localities'. (Pike, 2011, p17) These views may be different from adult views and it is necessary, as outlined above, to assess and use these views. One of the ways of doing this, and creating novel learning opportunities, is to explore locations both inside and outside the school using different subject lenses to provide alternative perspectives. Barnes and Shirley's (2007) 'strangely familiar' approach discussed above suggests that children first explore and then express the uniqueness of a place, integrating many areas of the curriculum, especially the arts such as poetry, art, and music. This involves using a variety of 'lenses', such as the musician, the film-maker, the poet, the artist or the dancer, but with control being passed to the pupils in selecting not only the perspective adopted, but also the resources, including ICT, to be used. The activity begins with a journey, and the initial journey itself could be part of using ICT to make it 'strange', such as showing them a video on the journey of a character setting the scene or posing a challenge. Alternatively, and perhaps even better, try other non-ICT approaches such as 'characters' joining the bus to tell their stories – most schools have at least one teacher who could be persuaded to dress up a pirate who could kidnap the bus and take it to his/her secret hiding place for buried treasure! Upon arrival the pupils can could consider which role(s), such as musician, dancer and so on (the subject lens, or combination of lenses), that they want to adopt to explore and report on their experience – although you will have to have the relevant equipment available (and charged!). Some possibilities are given in table 8.2 below:

Table 8.2 Exploring a 'strangely familiar' location – Lenses and ICT resources

Lens	ICT resource
The musician	• Sequencer • Keyboards • Digital recorders
The film-maker	• Digital camera (still and movie) • Digital editing software – e.g. Movie Maker • IWB for showing end product
The poet	• Word processor
The dancer	• Devise dance for the setting – perhaps using digital recordings of music from the musicians above • CD player • Digital camera (still and movie) to record and appraise performance
The artist	• Montage of digital pictures of odd / unique features of the local area – *everybody looks for the familiar and obvious things, why not collect images of the unexpected / strange features?*
The historian	• Podcasts or Vidcasts created of digital recordings (audio and/or video) of interviews with older members of the community who can provide first-hand experience and life stories of growing up in, or moving into, the area and different communities.
The scientist	• Use data loggers to measure temperature and other features of the setting

Graphicacy

Another geographical lens is provided by graphicacy which 'can be thought of as the sub-set of visual-spatial thinking that applies particularly to geography. It refers to the essentially pictorial ways, from photographs to diagrams and maps, in which we communicate spatial information about places, spaces and environments'. (Mackintosh, 2011, p7) At the end of Key Stage 2 this may involve using, for instance, Ordnance Survey (OS) maps and symbols, but preparation for this begins in the early years. ICT has an important role in this move from horizontal to vertical perspectives and from pictures to maps. In the first of these transitions Figure 8.1 (Mackintosh, 2011, p7) shows the contribution of digital images as the view change from early KS1 with

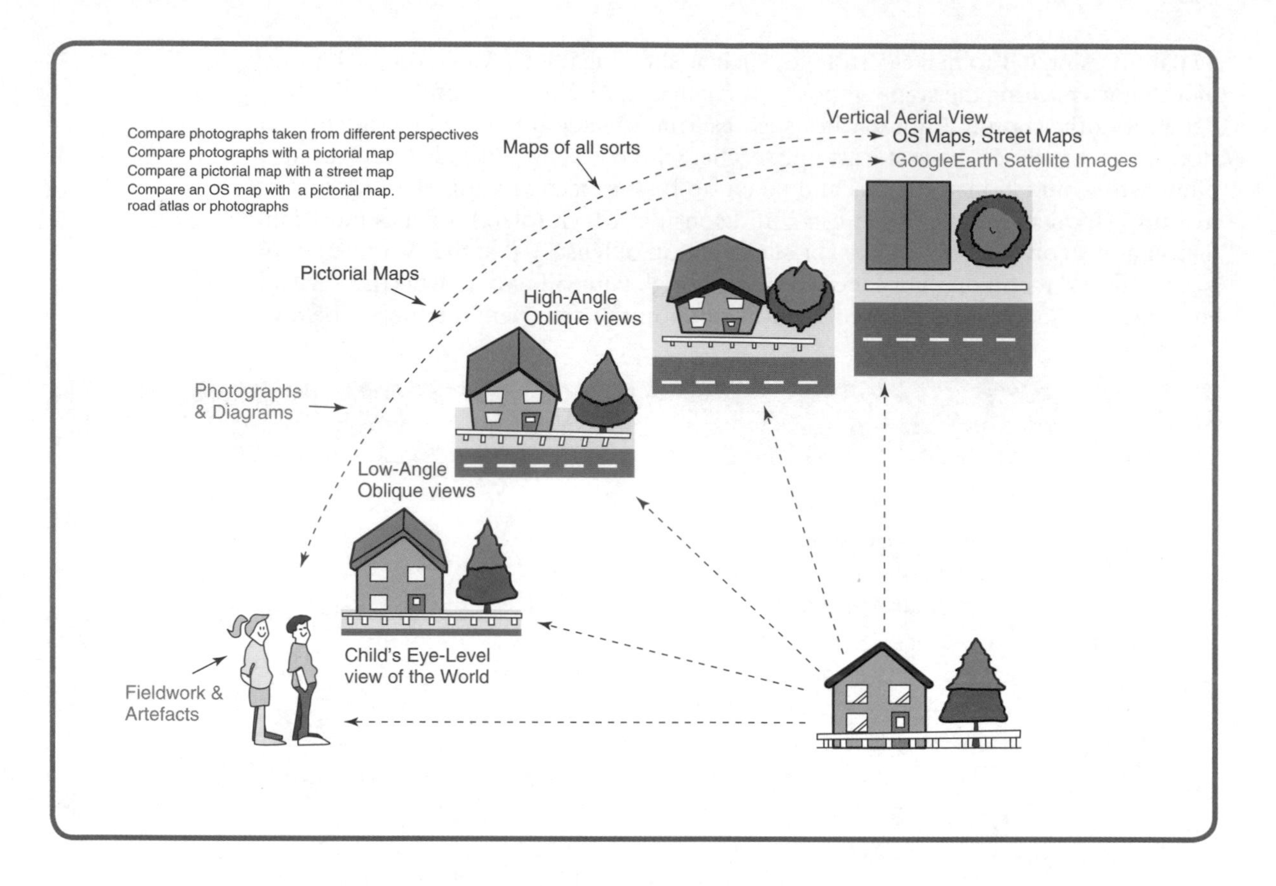

Figure 8.1

a horizontal child's eye view of real objects from ground level in field work, through to the end of KS2 with a symbolic representation on objects based on a vertical view.

In this transition, ICT devices such as digital cameras (comparing views from side and above of everyday objects, viewed on IWB or other devices), video cameras (panning from side view in an arc to above view) and websites (such as Google Earth or Google street view used with Google maps) can offer a unique set of facilities not offered by other resources.

Model of place

Another geographical lens is offered by an adaptation of Goodey's (1971) model of place. Figure 8.2 shows a revised version to reflect the experience of primary schools pupils. This new model extends the original but also incorporates specifically the impact of ICT, not present in the original model developed more than forty years ago. An integral part of the revised model reflects the fact that 'place' can now be a virtual concept. Pupils are very familiar with *real* places in other countries, but we are increasingly beginning to explore the educational potential of a range of *virtual* worlds – such as Second Life – particularly through gaming.

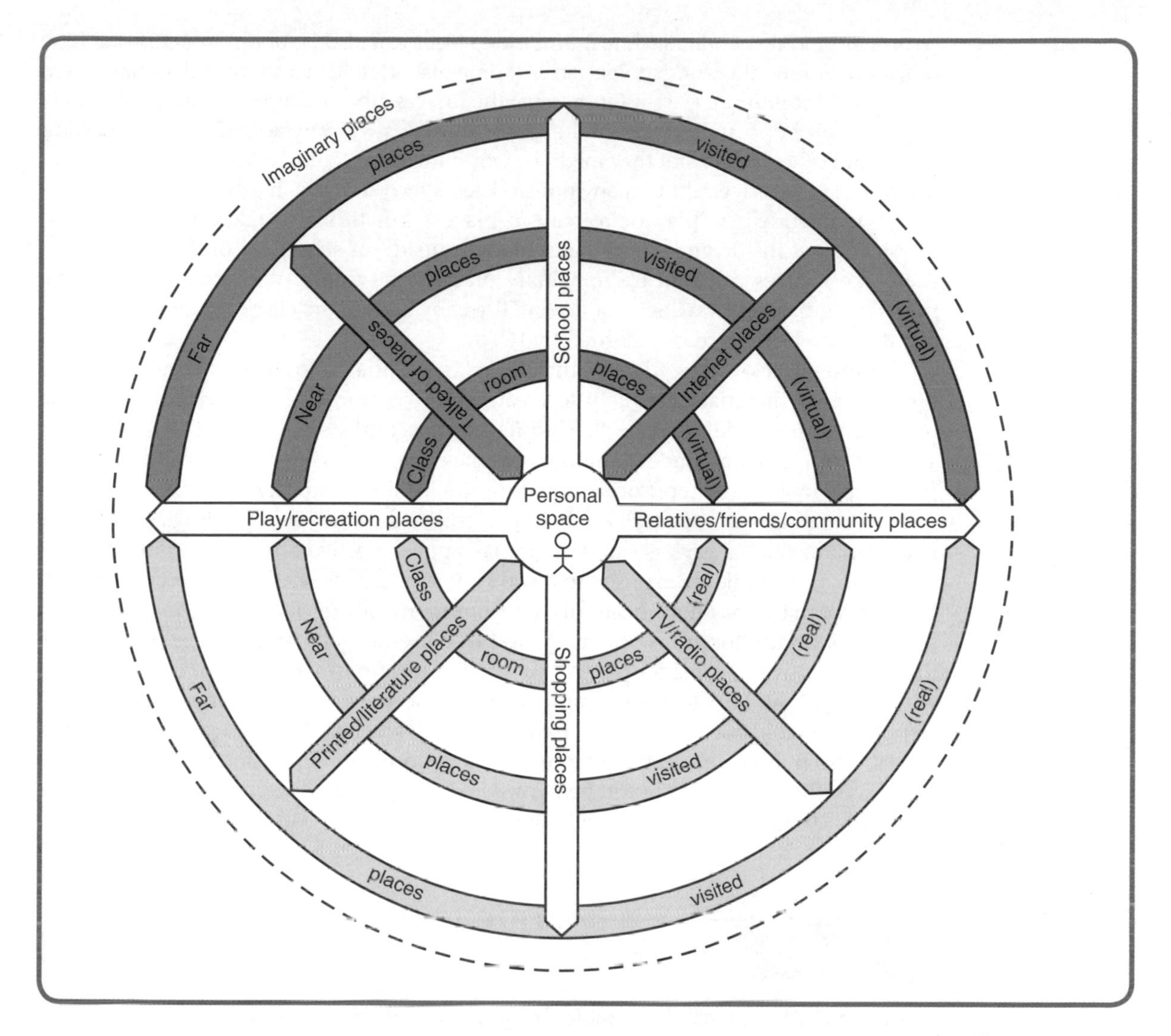

Figure 8.2 Model of place and ICT

This model takes as its starting point the premise that young children begin (and return to at will) their explorations from their own 'personal space' – be it in the classroom, home or elsewhere. The concentric circles moving outwards from the centre show an increasingly distant range of places moving from personal space to classroom places, near places and far places visited. The real places are in the bottom half of the circle, but the facility of ICT to 'visit' these places virtually, and at any time - even from within personal space - is shown in the top half of the circle. This takes account of the ability of a very young child to be based in their personal space (at home or in the classroom) and yet able to 'visit' a very faraway place on a PC or through videos of a family holiday (on TV, PC or a hosting service such as 'YouTube'), or those of their friends, members of their community or anybody who posts a video! As well as these recorded visits, others can take place in real time using ICT, through live video feeds, such as those from zoo websites (for example, San Diego) or city centres around the world. Such real time video feeds can also be useful in discussing time difference around the world as you can see some places are light and some dark (and often display the local time), even if (at present) the images are sometimes not as good quality as you might hope. Indeed, the quality of these images will vary according to connection speed, and other factors, but they might be worth the effort to use in lessons – and remember you can take screen shots at any time to keep a record or use in other lessons.

ICT is included in 'play or recreation places', but this also takes account of real physical play, inside and, more particularly, outside of school or on holiday. All of these experiences can lead to 'imaginary places'. The final outer circle, representing these 'imaginary places' does not *need* ICT, as any early years classroom will evidence, but they can be created or recorded by ICT.

The model also acknowledges that more traditional resources, such as books or other printed materials, can help to create a place (both real and imaginary) in the minds of young children. As well as printed stories, oral stories ('talked of places') can also contribute to the understanding of a place and can come from family members (who have lived elsewhere) or from within the local community.

The overall aim of the model to help you realise that the concept of place, and how it is formed, is not always as simple as it may appear, particularly with recent advances in technology. Pupils are exposed to a wide range of experiences and their current conceptions of place may have been formed from many of the views in the model. When planning work on locations, it may be useful to use the geographical lens provided by the model above to consider how to present the location in a variety of formats (both with and without ICT) to ensure pupils arrive at a secure and multi-dimensional understanding. What is not shown easily on the model is the role of the *people* in the various places, who pupils can meet and discuss the location with in real and virtual meetings. As always, the use of ICT should be because of its ability to do something faster, more efficiently or in a way that nothing else can.

ACTIVITY

In Chapter 6 we looked at a table showing how the features of ICT could be mapped against literacy activities. This table is repeated below but you need to add examples which demonstrate how ICT could be used in a topic-based approach including as many areas of the curriculum as appropriate to use the technology to its best effect.

Possible actions for which ICT provides potential and structure

Action	Meaning	Example
Composing	Ideas can be recorded accurately as they arise	
Editing	The data stored and displayed can be changed easily with no trace of the original	

(continued)

Action	Meaning	Example
Selecting	Choice of pre-existing resource or procedure can be made (e.g from a list)	
Comparing	Features of same object from different views or different items displayed can be compared	
Retrieving	Stored resources can easily be retrieved for use	
Apprehending	The display (text, images, sound, diagrams) makes it easier for students to see or interpret	
Focusing	Attention can be drawn to particular aspects of a process or representation	
Transforming	The way that the data are displayed can be changed	
Role playing	Activities can be carried out in a way which is similar to activity in the 'real world'	
Collating	The facility to bring together a variety of items from different sources into a single resource	
Sharing	The facility to communicate and interchange resources and ideas easily with others	
Annotating	Notes can be added to a process or representation at the time of use	
Repeating	An automated or stored process can be repeated at will	
Modelling	A process can be simulated by representing relationships between variables	
Cumulating	Building up a representation of knowledge in a progressive manner	
Revisiting	Repeating an activity or returning with a different focus	
Undoing	Reversing an action	
Questioning	Piece of dialogue requiring a response	
Prompting	Action or pviece of dialogue which suggests what someone should do	
Responding	Action which is contingent on a previous question/prompt	

Video conferencing

One of the ways that places (and people) can be visited in real time is through the use of videoconferencing, but it also has other uses across the primary curriculum. At present, it may not be used as much in the primary school as secondary, but the possibilities should not be ignored – although there is an obvious need for specific hardware (such as cameras) and software (such as Skype), as well as a good internet connection. In addition to other language opportunities we have discussed in earlier chapters, there is some evidence that videoconferencing may be useful in helping to teach modern foreign languages (MFL) and building links with secondary schools. In one research project, the secondary teacher of MFL taught a series of lessons (pre-planned with the primary teacher) to primary pupils while based in the secondary school classroom. The primary teacher ensured their class was managed effectively, but also, as a non-specialist, was able to join in the learning. Pritchard, Hunt and Barnes (2010, p211) suggest the benefits of videoconferencing for teachers and learners in all subjects are that it can:

- provide an authentic learning experience (experiencing the world outside the videoconferencing classroom);
- raise cultural awareness;
- provide access to experts (ability to communicate with authors, artists, specialist teachers etc.);
- improve social and communication skills (by developing listening and speaking skills);
- promote a measure of autonomy (break times were sometimes used to communicate with 'video pals').

Of course, another use of videoconferencing can be in sharing work or performances in other areas, such as music, with others in real time.

Music

When using a musical lens we need to examine the three fundamental process of music in the curriculum: performing, composing and appraisal (using musical vocabulary to discuss performances). The position of technology is long established within music teaching in primary schools, but this has largely focussed on equipment that helps to organise or manipulate sounds, rather than using more generic ICT equipment in music. From the earliest use of records, and more particularly radio, technology took the place of teachers to give pupils 'opportunities for enjoyment and learning [in music] which ordinary teachers could not expect to muster'. (Rainbow and Cox, 2006, p280) The influence of records and the radio was also significant in homes and wider society. This process was two-way in that technology used in society gradually took its place in schools. In more recent years, this has been reflected in technology developed primarily for the music industry, such as keyboards, audio recording and midi sequencers, become an important part of primary school music. In short, 'the history of technology in the classroom has been inextricably bound up with the adoption of technological tools used in wider society'. (Gall and Breeze, 2007, p42) As I write this, I am sure that by the time you read it a new device will have arrived which will become common in society, will take its place in the classroom and you will wonder why I did not mention it! It also seems likely that such changes are likely to happen more quickly. Nevertheless, at the time of writing, it is easy to record (audio and video), notate, sequence, replay and share music without sophisticated recording devices and associated technical skill that made this difficult in earlier times. This use of mobile devices also means that activities are not restricted to the school classroom, or even the school itself. They also allow pupils to do these things with or without adult support, depending on their level of experience with ICT. In addition, recordings can be made in HD quality with devices such as Flip Cams and ipod2s. These activities ('using ICT to capture, change and combine sounds' in the National Curriculum) are, however, perhaps the most apparent use of ICT in music teaching, and a musical lens presents other, less obvious, opportunities.

The English National Curriculum (KS2) for music states that pupils should be taught 'how time and place can influence the way music is created, performed and heard [for example, the effect of occasion and venue]'. We have already seen one example of this above with composition in a prehistoric cave, and this links well with the idea of located interaction outlined above, but also stems from the ideas in KS1 that pupils should learn 'how music is used for particular purposes [for example, for dance, as a lullaby]', which is often associated with a time or place. This idea of looking at the purpose of a composition as a composer is similar to thinking as an author in English work, who has to write for a particular audience. In a similar way, the composer (and author) has to consider the purpose of their work. For instance, is the work to communicate information (presentation), to encourage empathy (pictures and voices), to excite (sequencing a dance piece), to provide authenticity (recorded interview with someone who lived through the second world war) or provide a true record (video a dance or gym routine)? A musician will also make conscious choices about the instruments or sound sources (ICT tools) to be used to gain the required effect, just as a pupil or teacher should do the same with ICT resources.

ICT and all that jazz

The musical lens also suggests that musical compositional techniques can offer a useful framework for classroom organisation using ICT. The purpose of this framework is similar to other examples above, in that as well as providing a tool for classroom analysis (in teaching and research), it also allows you to consider if you are using all possible methods of classroom organisation within and between lessons. Although based on work with IWBs, the framework can also be applied to other ICT tools and resources. The analogies resulted from ideas discussed within a research team and the following is a summary only – see Beauchamp et al., (2010) for full details. When observing lessons in a research project we noticed that, although all lessons were planned in advance, there were occasions within lessons where teachers and learners moved outside the constraints of a pre-determined lesson orchestration and began to improvise. These episodes varied in length, but 'the musical analogy is a powerful one in characterising the manipulation of features in the classroom setting in order to generate activity or 'performance' which leads to learning'. (Beauchamp et al., 2010, p145) Zack (2000) suggested that the jazz metaphor could be used to examine and classify speech against musical genres and how these compared these to Konitz's stages (cited in Zack, 2000). Table 8.3 (from Beauchamp et al., 2010) shows how both could be related the ICT use in the classroom by mapping against Beauchamp and Kennewell's (2010) categories of classroom interaction and interactions with ICT.

Table 8.3 Musical genres and classroom interactions

Music genre	Konitz's stages	Communication metaphor	Category of interaction	Interaction with ICT
Classical – *minimal improvisation*	Interpretation	Formal pre-de fined, linear	Authoritative	Factual recall, following standard procedure or browsing fixed hypertext
Traditional jazz/ swing – *constrained improvisation within a well-structured context*	Embellish-ment	Predictable but flexible scripts; strict turn taking and use of adjacency pairs – highly predictable statement and response pairs	Dialectic	Constructing product to specified brief, involving selection of options and sources
Bebop – *extensive modification of the tune using wide range of notes and rhyikms and some modification to harmonic structure*	Variation	Complex, but structured conversation	Dialogic	Developing product, requiring information seeking, hypothesis testing, comparison and elaboration of material
Postbop/free jazz – *maximal improvisation of the structure, content and rules of improvisation – 'functional anarcky'*	Improvisation	Emergent, spontaneous, interactive, mutually constructed conversation	Synergistic	Open problem-solving or creating product involving identification of context/material, analysis, reflection

Some of the elements of this table will be familiar from earlier chapters, but the key distinction is that we are now labelling unplanned moments in a lesson, when serendipity provides the stimulus for a new direction. This stimulus can come from both teachers and pupils or even ICT – for instance, the discovery of a new feature of the IWB or a piece of software. Just because the resultant activity is not planned, it does not mean the opportunity should be missed. In fact, having the confidence to see the potential of unplanned opportunities for learning, and to use them, is the sign of a good teacher.

Table 8.3 also provides an opportunity to think about the lessons you are planning. Are they all 'classical' or do you have some which have more of a swing to them?

Video Stimulated Reflective Dialogue (VSRD)

It was noted above that it is possible to record musical (but also, for example, PE, dance and science investigations) 'performances' using audio and video. This is particularly important in music, as the video recording allows you to look at the way instruments were played, or beaters were used to achieve a particular sound or effect, as well as listen to the end result. The use of video to enable pupils to reflect on both their work and their learning, has been used in research and is labelled video stimulated reflective dialogue (VSRD), or variations of this. In this technique, which can be used in classroom assessment as well as research, video recordings are made of activities and then used to stimulate dialogue and discussion. The video helps children to remember what actually took place (particularly important for younger children), but also allows them (and teachers) to see what others were doing a time which they may have missed. Depending on the software, the features of ICT make it possible for pupils to view the movie immediately after the event (for instance by plugging a Flip Cam into a laptop), to move backwards and forwards within the movie, and replay either the whole movie or a small part of it as many times as necessary to clarify events or to focus attention on different things.

CASE STUDY

In a recent research project with Key Stage two pupils (Salisbury et al., 2011; Beauchamp et al., 2009),VSRD was used alongside a range of other visual elicitation methods to try and assess the understanding of science concepts with pupils for whom English was an Additional Language (EAL) – in this case with Polish as the home language. The pupils were video recorded by researchers as they undertook a range of practical science activities which focused on 'Forces' as a topic. One of these was trying to drop the ball into a bucket as they ran past it, without throwing it in or exerting a downward force. Coloured cones were placed on the ground at intervals both before and after the bucket. The digital recordings were shown to the pupils in their groups as part of an interview process –where the video stimulated the dialogue.

At the beginning of the interview, the researcher used the mouse to control the video. It quickly became evident, however, that the Y4/6 pupils involved were very keen to take control of the movie and one child spontaneous took the mouse and used it to move to a spot in the video to show the others an incident he had spotted. After this, other pupils also took the mouse and moved backwards and forwards through the movie by dragging the cursor, as well as pausing to look at specific instances. This was a particularly powerful tool as the HD quality of the video allowed a good still frame shot. It was in this way that the pupils discovered for themselves about their relative positions in relation to the bucket when they dropped the ball. They soon realised that although they thought they had dropped the ball over the top of the bucket when successfully getting it in, in reality they had dropped it slightly before, very near one of the cones.

(continued)

Although the main purpose of the video have been to assess their understanding of the topic, by taking control of the video and using the provisionality and interactive features of the recording the pupils also co-constructed their own understanding of an important part of the topic.

Incidentally, the fact that they were looking at themselves and video in the video was a great source of motivation (and amusement at times!) for pupils.

As with many aspects of ICT, there are some technical issues which need to be considered when making the video. For instance, you need to consider where to place the camera so that all participants are seen (on a tall or short stand or none at all?), will the a battery last long enough without a power supply, do we need an additional microphone and how to ensure that the camera view is not blocked. In reality, as this would probably take place focusing on a small group (such as a group performance), rather than the whole class, most of these issues will not be a cause for concern. It should also be remembered that any recordings can also be used as evidence of work or can be added to a digital or e-portfolio (see p. 86).

Introducing new resources

Before we move to the final chapter, we need to consider an important issue we have so far ignored, that of how to introduce new ICT resources or skills. We have already considered that as digital natives pupils arrive at school with many ICT skills, sometimes in advance of the teacher. No matter how much training is available, the reality is that ICT is only one area where teachers need new understanding and skills and it will have to compete with other school priorities and new national initiatives. Throughout this book we have discussed the growing democracy in the primary school classroom and the potential benefits and we will return to this later. To end this chapter, however, let us consider a scenario which represents one possible approach to the above issues.

SCENARIO

School A has a wireless network which the headteacher was careful to ensure covered all the school grounds when it was installed. This enabled pupils to gain access to the school network as well as the internet. As the pupils had been using ICT since reception they were very confident in using laptops but the school had decided to invest in some new technology and had bought a set of ipod 2s, which have a camera in. At a staff meeting the ICT co-ordinator suggested that

(*continued*)

these should just be given to the pupils and they should be asked to explore them during their work on habitats in the school grounds, which, even though it was an inner-city school, included a small 'Forest School' area. After much discussion about whether relevant IT 'skills' should be taught in advance, the rest of the staff agreed to try this with the two classes, one in Y2 and one is Y6, who were investigating habitats as part of their work on the science scheme of work. They would discuss the outcomes at the next staff meeting. The main concern of the teachers was that they were not all familiar with the technology themselves. To allay their fears, the ICT co-ordinator and those staff who had used similar technology showed the others the basics of using the device.

The only advanced preparation that was done was to ensure that the wireless code had been entered so that all the devices connected automatically to the school network – and that all devices were fully charged! In the first lesson they were used, the Y2 class teacher gave the class a challenge to try and find places in the school grounds where 'creatures' lived. They would have to report back at the end of the session and they could use their ICT devices as they wanted – or not at all. The Y6 class were set the challenge of finding, identifying and recording the habitats of as many living 'creatures' in the school grounds as possible using the technology in the same way. Both teachers asked pupils to work in small groups and gave each group a ipod2. After the initial excitement (and warnings about using carefully and sharing!) the classes went outside into the school grounds.

The teachers moved between groups as necessary, but were surprised to see that the pupils quickly managed to work out how to use the camera ('poke' the camera icon) and even found they could take movies ('poke' on the icon of the video camera). The older children quickly found the internet icon and started using it to search for information via the wireless connection. One Y6 group asked the teacher for the school email address so that they could send a picture, but this had not yet been set up on the devices – although the teacher noted that this needed to be done for next time they were used. Both teachers were surprised how many of the pupils already knew how to use the devices and showed others. Coincidentally both classes were outside at the same time and some Y2 pupils also asked others in Y6 how to do things.

At the end of the lesson the pupils returned to the classrooms to discuss and share what they had found. All groups had used the camera on the devices and many had found other features such as sound recorders, the internet and the notes page to record text. The main problem was that the pictures and sound files were on the devices and, as these were small, it was not possible to share easily with others – although one teacher later realised that they could have installed the Dropbox app on the ipod and then connected to this on the classroom PC and IWB for whole class use. However, all the pupils had completed

(continued)

their challenge and found a range of habitats and creatures. At the next staff meeting, the teachers reported their surprise at the speed at which pupils had learned to use the devices and how they had found features which the teachers did not know about – such as the sound recorder. They reported that if the email was set up it would be easy to send files to an email address which could be accessed on the IWB for the whole class to see. Also, if the files could be added to the school network this would also help. The first of these was easy to do, but the security settings on the school network made the second harder, but worth investigating. The main topic of discussion was how advanced the pupils seemed in comparison with the staff. The key questions discussed were:

- are we as teachers underestimating our pupils, and;
- are we holding them back with our own fears about technology?

What do you think?

WHAT WOULD YOU DO?

One child in the Y6 class asked if the Facebook app could be downloaded onto the ipod. When asked why, it was because it was easy to upload a picture of the habitat there and then it could be shared. As the Y6 pupil should not be old enough to have a Facebook page (even though you know many in your class do), how do you proceed? Do you discuss with the pupil or the whole class?

SUMMARY

In this chapter we have considered how to approach cross-curricular teaching using a range of subject lenses to encourage unique approaches to learning and teaching. We have not covered all subject lenses but I hope that the examples provided will encourage you to consider how the pedagogies of different subject areas can stimulate an alternative approach. This does not mean that proven pedagogies should be neglected, but rather that sometimes a fresh approach can reinvigorate both teacher and pupils. Within these approaches the use of ICT remains selective and should exploit its unique potential.

In the next, and final, chapter we will move from the present to what may happen in the future as new technologies take their place in society and in school.

References

Adams, D. (2011), 'Music-making at Prehistoric sites' presented at Leading Music Education International Conference, Don Wright Faculty of Music, The University of Western Ontario. 29 May–1 June 2011.

Barnes, J. (2007), *Cross-curricular Learning 3–14*, London: Paul Chapman Publishing.

Barnes, J. and Shirley, I. (2007), 'Strangely familiar: cross-curricular and creative thinking in teacher education', *Improving Schools*, 10(2), pp162–79.

Becta (2002), *ICT supporting teaching: developing effective practice*, Coventry: Becta.

Beauchamp, G. (2010), 'Knowledge and understanding of the world', in Palaiologou, I. (ed). *The Early Years Foundation Stage: Theory and Practice*, London: Sage, pp167–77.

Beauchamp, G., Kennewell, S., Tanner, H. and Jones, S. (2010), 'Interactive whiteboards and all that jazz: the contribution of musical metaphors to the analysis of classroom activity with interactive technologies', *Technology, Pedagogy and Education*, 19: 2, 143–17.

Beauchamp, G., Ellis, C., Haughton, C. and Salisbury, J. (2009), 'The use of ICT and video stimulated reflective dialogue (VSRD) in assessing conceptual understanding of science in primary schools children with English as an additional language (EAL)', to be presented at BERA conference, Manchester, 3–5 September 2009.

Bennett, R., Hamill, A. and Pickford, T. (2007), *Progression in Primary ICT*, Abingdon: David Fulton.

Brindley, S. (2000), 'ICT and Literacy,' in Gamble, N. and Easingwood, N. (eds) (2000), *ICT and Literacy*, London: Continuum. pp11–18.

Cage, John (1961), *Silence: Lectures and Writings*, Middletown, Conn.: Wesleyan University Press, reprinted London: Marion Boyars, 1999.

Churches, A. (2009), *Bloom's Digital Taxonomy*, **http://tinyurl.com/2dr6f3v**

Cockburn, A.D. and Littler, G. (2008), *Mathematical Misconceptions: A Guide for Primary Teachers*, London: Sage.

Drews, D. (2005), 'Children's mathematical errors and misconceptions: perspectives on the teacher's role', in Hansen, A. (ed.) (2005), *Children's Errors in Mathematics: Understanding, Misconceptions*, Exeter: Learning Matters, pp14–21.

Engeström, Y. (2001), 'Expansive learning at work: Toward an activity theoretical reconceptualization', *Journal of Education and Work*, 14, 133–56.

Gall, M. and Breeze, N. (2007), 'The sub-culture of music and ICT in the classroom', *Technology, Pedagogy and Education*, 16: 1, 41–56.

Hall, D. (2010), *The ICT Handbook for Primary Teachers: A Guide for Students and Professionals*, London: Routledge.

Harlen, W. and Qualter, A. (2007) *The Teaching of Science in Primary Schools*, 4th edition, London: David Fulton.

Hellen, M. (2010), 'Information handling and adaptive expertise', *Education and Information Technology*, 16, pp107–22.

Hollins, M. and Whitby, V. (2001) *Progression in Primary Science: A Guide to the Nature and Practice of Science in Key Stages 1 and 2,* Second Edition, London: David Fulton.

Mackintosh, M. (2011), 'Graphicacy for life', *Primary Geographer*, June 2011, 6–8.

Robert McCormick (2004): 'ICT and pupil assessment', *Curriculum Journal*, 15:2, 115–37.

McDougall, A. (2001), 'Guest editorial: assessing learning with ICT', *Journal of Computer Assisted Learning* (2001), 17(3), pp 223–26.

McFarlane, A. (2000), 'Communicating meaning – reading and writing in a multimedia world', in Gamble, N. and Easingwood, N. (eds), (2000), *ICT and Literacy*, London: Continuum, pp19–24.

Nunes, T. (2001), 'British research on the development of numeracy concepts', in Askew, M. and Brown, M. (eds) (2001), *Teaching and Learning Primary Numeracy: Policy, Practice and Effectiveness: A Review of British Research for the British Educational Research Association in Conjunction with the British Society for Research in the Learning of Mathematics*.

Ofsted (2008a), *ICT In Primary and Secondary Schools: Ofsted's Findings 2005/07* London: Oftsed.

Ofsted (2008b), *Mathematics: Understanding the Score*, London: Oftsed.

Pike, S. (2011), 'Children, locality and the future', *Primary Geographer*, March 2011, 17–19.

Pritchard, A., Hunt, M. and Barnes, A. (2010), 'Case study investigation of a videoconferencing experiment in primary schools, teaching modern foreign languages', *The Language Learning Journal*, 38:2, 209–20.

Rainbow, B. and Cox, G. (2006), *Music in Educational Thought and Practice*, Woodbridge: Boydell.

Rudd, A. and Tyldesley, A. (2006), *Literacy and ICT in the Primary School: A Creative Approach to English*, London: David Fulton.

Salisbury, J., Ellis, C., Beauchamp, G. and Haughton, C. (2011), 'What's occurring? The what, why, how and when of research capacity building in a modest pilot project with EAL learners and science', *Welsh Journal of Education*, 15(1), pp46–65.

Schafer., R. M (1994), *Soundscape. Our Sonic environment and the tuning of the world*, New York: Knopf.

Summers, M., Kruger, C. and Mant, J. (1998), 'Teaching electricity effectively in the primary school: a case study', *International Journal of Science Education*, 20:2, 153–72.

Turner-Bisset, R. *Creative Teaching: History in the Primary Classroom*, London: David Fulton.

Wenger, E. (1998), *Communities of Practice: Learning, Meaning, and Identity*, Cambridge: Cambridge University Press.

Useful websites

To find some live web cameras around the UK: **http://gouk.about.com/od/picturegalleries/tp/UK_webcams.htm**

CHAPTER 9

Postscript: The Future

Perhaps the only thing we know for certain about the future of ICT is that we do not know what will happen! One of the guiding principles of this book has been that teachers should not be driven by the need to master a particular technology,but instead should examine what it has to offer in developing effective pedagogy. Indeed, there is a fundamental question about whether the future in education should be led by technology (technological determinism) or whether teachers (and pupils) should lead the development of technology? There is a problem in advocating the second, even if it is infinitely preferable, in that the driving force behind much technology is the needs or industry or society. This leads us to consider the view of Facer and Sandford (2010, p76) who propose that 'researching the future cannot simply be a case of producing a set of predictions of what "will happen" as though this were beyond the intervention of individuals or societies. Nor can it simply be a case of discussing what we "want" or "will make" happen, as though there were no prior contexts to shape our actions'. They continue to cite Bell's (1997, p.73) options of 'possible, probable, and preferable' futures: 'what can or could be (the possible), what is likely to be (the probable), and what ought to be (the preferable)'. Within these options, it is *probable* that the technological needs of industry will continue to drive the development of technology, but this does not mean that it is *preferable*. Indeed, this is one of a series of such dilemmas that could affect the future of ICT in education and even education itself – you only need to consider the on-going debate about the content of the curriculum or the current debate about 'Free' schools. This does not mean, however, that ICT developments driven by industry are a bad thing. Many devices, particularly the IWB, have their roots in industrial settings and have been successfully adopted in education. For the remainder of this chapter, however, we will consider what might be *possible*.

In the research literate there has been much debate about whether ICT will transform pedagogy (for example, Somekh and Davies, 1991), or if there is such thing as an ICT pedagogy, but there has been little consistent findings that new pedagogies have emerged – although there is some evidence that the IWB may be an exception. Indeed, the whole concept of one ICT pedagogy may prove a distraction. I have suggested previously (Beauchamp, 2006) that in primary school there may actually be many ICT pedagogies that emerge as teachers view learning and teaching through a variety of subject lenses. What I hope has emerged in the preceding chapters is that these pedagogies, regardless of the technology used, should only use ICT if it does something better, quicker or more effectively than other resources, or if it can reinforce ideas by offering a unique range of different perspectives using different modes and media.

At present we are mainly talking about these pedagogies being employed in a school setting, but another factor which will become important as primary schools move away from fixed PCs and laptops (though Cloud and other technologies), is that ICT can enable learning and teaching outside the bounds of the classroom, both in Early Years and throughout the primary school. By allowing access to a range of resources (both work files and programs), the physical classroom will increasingly become only one of a range of settings for learning – including virtual environments below.

Perhaps we should frame our thinking about the future of ICT by considering its past. For some years now, ICT has fundamentally been concerned with information, communication and technology, or increasingly with technologies. Information on its own is of limited use, but primary school pupils can now access it quicker and in a wider variety of formats and places. They are also able to use it in a variety of ways (such as in presentations, pieces of writing, art work, blogs or web sites), but this does not necessarily mean they *understand* it. Therefore the role of the teacher as scaffolder, mentor and facilitator will always remain vital, even if the speed of access and tools used by pupils become faster and more sophisticated. Indeed, in this context the role of the teacher may become more, not less, important as a mediator between the technology and the pupil. This communication between teacher and pupil, however, is only one of many modes of communication we have seen throughout this book. If anything, communication may be the most important aspect of ICT for teachers and pupils in the future. It is, however, what is communicated and why that is most important. Perhaps in the medium term, ICT as a 'label' will be replaced to reflect changing priorities? We could conjecture that the communication and sharing of understanding and multi-disciplinary ideas (within and between schools) through the use of technologies is a more accurate reflection of what happens in the primary school, even today, and this is likely to increase in the future. We have already conjectured above about where this will take place (for instance in a virtual classroom or from home), but this is less important than how and why it happens and who makes it happen. A more radical suggestion is that 'ICT' will disappear altogether as it becomes the equivalent today of paper and pen. This 'ubiquitous computing' is part of a view of technology in which 'computing technology is so embedded in theworld that it "disappears"'. (O'Malley and Stanton, 2006, p2) This view is part of a virtuality continuum (Milgram and Kishino 1994 cited in O'Malley and Stanton, 2006) which may come to be important in education:

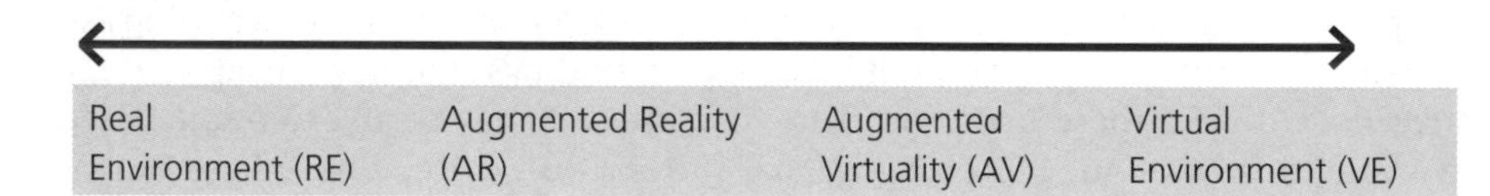

We have already considered purely virtual worlds, but the area between this and the real world is increasingly becoming a zone where technology could help pupils explore a range of environments, using the features of technology to good effect. O'Malley and Stanton (2006, p8) explain that 'whereas in virtual reality (VR) the goal is often to immerse the user in a computational world, in AR the physical world is augmented with digital information. … AR is where, for example, video images of real scenes are overlaid with 3D graphics. In augmented virtuality, displays of a 3D virtual world (possibly immersive) are overlaid with video feeds from the real world'. It is easy to imagine that if such technology (available in some forms today in rides at entertainment parks for example) was incorporated into teaching situations a host of new opportunities would arise.

Nevertheless, as stated already, even if 'ICT' does disappear, and new environments do become available, until computers can interpret not only human emotions, but also use their intuition to formulate a range of responses based on knowledge of the child, the importance of the relationship between teacher and pupils will remain. Throughout this book I have tried to convey the primary classroom as a partnership, where pupils take an active role in co-constructing knowledge and understanding, using a range of tools (including ICT) as appropriate. Access to these tools and equipping pupils to use them may remain the role of the teacher (or the school) in the first instance, but this should pass to the pupils as they move through the primary school. It is thus important that pupils understanding how they themselves learn, otherwise known as metacognition. There are many definitions of this term and we will adopt a broad definition as learning how to learn. In any definition, however, we are faced with the idea that,as well as a generic understanding of how they learn, pupils also need to learn how to learn with ICT (and perhaps other subjects in the primary school). As this would be an individual process, it could be argued that pupils, when supported by teachers, would need time to develop this understanding, and that it would develop as pupils move through the primary school.

In the current climate of accountability such an approach may seem an ideal, but if we are to take personalised learning seriously, and ICT is an important enabler in this regard, we need to be prepared to make radical changes to the primary school culture. In this context, the role of school leadership and management is central in facilitating the vision. A simple delineation between the two roles is that management is doing the job right and leadership is doing the right job. (Beauchamp and Harvey, 2006) This distinction between strategic and operational tasks/skills could actually be shared with pupils, who are, after all, hopefully the main beneficiaries of changes, but should also have some views in these matters. It may be that pupils assume some of this responsibility through school councils or other outlets for pupil voice. This may be especially important if we believe in the concept of digital natives, as discussed earlier, who have well developed skills in, and experience of, ICT in its many forms. Not only are primary pupils likely to be familiar with new technologies as they emerge, but also they also may see the potential for learning with them - 'but you can do that quicker / easier with the ... I have at home'. In other words they may be in a good position to advise not only on the right job, but also how to do it right!

It may be, however, that none of the above really matters if we take a more radical step and consider if we need ICT at all? Effective learning and teaching took place before ICT and we need to be sure that we (pupils and teachers) are using ICT for a good reason and not just because it is there. I hope that this book has helped to convince you that we *do* need ICT and has helped you to consider why, when and how it can work best in the primary school with *all* pupils. In chapter 1 I suggested that ICT can offer a range of unique features to teachers and learners, which are not available using other means. Whether or not pupils experience these unique features remains in your hands as teachers are gatekeepers to the technology. I hope that this book has helped to convince you not only to open the gate to everybody, but also to open it in many different ways!

References

Beauchamp, G. (2006), 'New technologies and 'new teaching': a process of evolution?' in *Changing Teaching and Learning in the Primary School*, ed. Webb, R. Open University Press. pp81–91.

Beauchamp, G. and Harvey, J. (2006), 'It's one of those scary areas': Leadership and management of music in primary schools', *British Journal of Music Education* 23(1), pp5–22.

Bell W. (1997), *Foundations of Futures Studies.* London: Transaction Publishers.

Facer. K. and Sandford, R. (2010),' The next 25 years? future scenarios and future directions for education and technology', *Journal of Computer Assisted Learning* (2010), 26, pp74–93.

O'Malley, C. and Stanton, D. (2006), *Literature Review in Learning with Tangible Technologies*, London: Future-lab.

Somekh, B. and Davies, R. (1991) 'Towards a pedagogy for information technology', *The Curriculum Journal*, 2, pp. 153–170.

Index